MANAGER MECHANICS

Other Titles in the Capital Career & Personal Development Series:

THE 10 LENSES: Your Guide to Living & Working in a Multicultural World by Mark A. Williams

BE HEARD THE FIRST TIME: The Woman's Guide to Powerful Speaking by Susan Miller

MENTAL AGILITY: The Path to Persuasion by Robert L. Jolles

MILLION DOLLAR NETWORKING: The Sure Way to Find, Grow and Keep Your Business by Andrea Nierenberg

THE NEW TALK POWER: The Mind-Body Way to Speak like a Pro by Natalie H. Rogers

NONSTOP NETWORKING: How to Improve Your Life, Luck, and Career by Andrea Nierenberg

NOW WHAT DO I DO? The Woman's Guide to a New Career by Jan Cannon

THE POWER OF HANDSHAKING: For Peak Performance Worldwide by Robert E. Brown and Dorothea Johnson

THE SAVVY PART-TIME PROFESSIONAL: How to Land, Create, or Negotiate the Part-Time Job of Your Dreams by Lynn Berger

SOLD! Direct Marketing for the Real Estate Pro by Louis K. Geller

YOUR IDENTITY ZONES: Who Am I? Who Are You? How Do We Get Along? by Mark A. Williams

Save 25% when you order any of these and other fine Capital titles from our Web site: www.capital-books.com.

MANAGER MECHANICS

People Skills for the
First-Time Manager

Eric P. Bloom

Capital Career & Personal Development Series

CAPITAL
BOOKS, INC.
Sterling, Virginia

Capital Books, Inc.
P.O. Box 605
Herndon, Virginia 20172-0605

ISBN 10: 1-933102-31-4 (alk. paper)
ISBN 13: 978-1-933102-31-3

Library of Congress Cataloging-in-Publication Data

Library of Congress Cataloging-in-Publication Data

Bloom, Eric P.
    Manager mechanics : people skills for the first-time manager / Eric P. Bloom.
        p. cm. -- (Capital business series)
    ISBN 1-933102-31-4 (alk. paper)
    1. Supervision of employees. 2. Interpersonal communication. 3. Management. I. Title. II. Series.

    HF5549.12.B625 2006
    658.3'02—dc22

                                                    2006019994

Printed in the United States of America on acid-free paper that meets the American National Standards Institute Z39-48 Standard.

First Edition

10 9 8 7 6 5 4 3 2 1

To Jonathan and Emily

CONTENTS

ACKNOWLEDGMENTS

I would like to thank the many people who assisted me in the creation of this book. Your help, suggestions, guidance, and support are truly appreciated. In particular, I would like to thank Emily Bloom and Jonathan Bloom for suggesting various topics for the book and for their general inspiration, David Ossam for his advice, Mandy Tom for suggesting I write the book, and Denise Boulanja for proofreading the original manuscript.

PREFACE

∽ Nobody Reads the Preface;
But Maybe You Should Read This One ∽

How about that? I got you to read the preface.

On a serious note, this book took twenty-five years and four months to write. The twenty-five years represents my business experience working within small, medium, and large companies. Over that time, I have been an individual contributor, a project leader, a manager of individual contributors, and a manager of managers.

Over the years, I worked for a few great managers, a number of good managers, and a few, well, not good managers. From the great managers, I learned about leadership, courage, professional competence, and the many other traits that we aspire to attain. From the good managers, I learned about solid management practice, the importance of understanding your job, and the reasons for doing it well. From the less-than-good managers, I learned how not to manage, how not to treat your team, and how it feels to be poorly managed. In all cases, I observed their actions and learned from their managerial triumphs and failures. From these experiences, I gained the knowledge needed to become a manager myself and ultimately to write this book.

The four months alludes to the time it took to put pen to paper (OK, put fingers to keyboard. I was going for the Ernest Hemmingway thing and it didn't work. Well, live and learn).

My goal with this book is to provide you, a new manager, with knowledge that will help you grow professionally, help you help your subordinates to grow professionally, and help you contribute to your company's success.

My hope is that you find this book to be a fast read, very informative, and a little bit entertaining. Should you want to contact me regarding this book, I can be reached via EricPBloom@ManagerMechanics.com. Happy reading, good managing, and good luck.

Eric P. Bloom

INTRODUCTION

～ What Is Manager Mechanics? ～

Manager Mechanics is based on the core set of personal traits, skills, and knowledge needed to be a great manager.

The personal traits include a willingness to take on responsibility, provide leadership, and act decisively, and a desire to treat others with respect, honesty, and integrity.

The skills include the ability to communicate, delegate, hire quality people, teach and mentor staff, organize meetings, run projects, properly set expectations, follow directions, give directions, and instill confidence in others.

The knowledge includes an understanding of office politics, budgeting, human-resource-related activities, planning, forecasting, and a working knowledge of the area you are managing.

This book has been designed to address these and other areas in an informative, fun, and fast manner. It can be read quickly. I hope you enjoy the book and enjoy being a manager.

～ Some Specifics ～

At various times in the book, I generically refer to the "Human Resources (HR) department" and the "finance department." In large companies, these departments may each have hundreds of people, and in small companies, there may be a single person who performs both functions. In either case, when I suggest that you speak with the HR or finance department, I simply mean that you should speak to the person in your company knowledgeable and/or responsible for these business functions.

Regarding the he/she debate: While writing this book, I tried to use both genders equally. In other words, I used he/him examples as often as she/her examples. I did this because I have found that men and women make equally good and equally bad managers. For me personally, my best manager was a woman and my worst manager was a man. The reason that I am speaking about this at all is because as a writer (and as a manager), I try to be fair and even in all ways.

The "Training Guide" at the end of the book has been designed to assist training professionals, HR generalists, and individual readers by featuring individual chapter outlines, including each chapter's theme, key concepts, and questions for discussion.

For training professionals and HR generalists, the outlines provide a framework for presenting the material as part of a management-training curriculum. For individual readers, the "Discussion Questions" can act as food for thought. As a new manager, thinking about scenarios like these can better prepare you for the times when these scenarios happen for real (yeah, sorry, these things really do happen).

The book's accompanying website, www.ManagerMechanics.com, contains additional training materials, training suggestions, and links to other high-quality management training materials, books, and organizations.

CHAPTER 1

FOOD FOR THOUGHT FOR A NEW MANAGER

～ Have Kids? You Have All the Management Training You Need ～

Believe it or not, caring for your children is good management training. As a parent, you learn to praise and discipline your children, as well as provide guidance, direction, leadership, and a pleasant living environment. You teach your children new skills and give them additional training via teachers and trainers. You make sure they have the supplies needed to perform various tasks, like crayons, scissors, and paper. You teach them to minimize unneeded risks, like running with scissors and looking both ways before crossing the street. You learn that each child is an individual with his or her own personality, likes, dislikes, motivations, skills, and abilities. Lastly, you realize the need to treat each child as an individual, the importance of being part of a family, and the responsibility that being part of a family brings.

Another thing that a parent quickly realizes (or at least I did) is that you don't have all the answers. As a parent, you find that you must learn new specific skills, like changing diapers, food preparation, and family budgeting. You also learn the importance of decision making. Questions such as, "What to make for dinner?" "Does the child need to see the doctor?" "Which school is best?" "Should a child be punished?" "Is it OK for my child to go to a party if the parents are not home?" have to be answered. You also have to learn how to react properly when your children whine, yell in restaurants, throw their food, and complain about their siblings.

Now let's talk about being a manager.

As a manager, you have to lead and motivate your staff, administer praise and discipline, provide guidance, provide work direction, and facilitate employee growth through on-the-job training and formalized instruction.

Being a good manager also requires good judgment, fairness, and the ability to foster teamwork among your employees. Get the message?

∽ Caring About Your Group Is Half the Battle, but Not the Whole Story ∽

A person newly promoted to manager asked me, "How do I know that I'll be a good manager?" He went on to say that he liked the people in his group and wanted to do a good job as their new leader. I told him that caring about his people and wanting to be a good manager is half the battle. There are of course many other aspects of effective management, but this is a good start.

> I have seen time and time again that the best managers are those who want to treat their people fairly and honestly.

I have also seen very capable, qualified managers who performed poorly and were disliked by their subordinates and peers because they didn't care about the motivation, education, or interests of their subordinates. That said, being a good manager is more than just wanting to be a manager. It requires specific skills that may be very different from what you learned in school. Beyond the technical knowledge associated with the group you are managing, there are also three basic types of skills required to be an effective and competent manager: interpersonal skills, business skills, and good judgment. Interpersonal skills are your abilities to personally relate to your boss, your peers, and your subordinates. Business skills are the learned management tasks required by your company such as budgeting, salary planning, and giving performance reviews. Good judgment is your ability to respond appropriately when various situations, issues, and problems arise. This book does its best to address these three areas. In all honesty, however, some business skills can be learned from a book, but interpersonal skills are primarily based on personal persona, and good judgment is often best learned through experience, in other words, trial and error.

∾ Your Team Doesn't Have to Like You, but They Do Have to Respect You ∾

Another thing that a parent and manager have in common is the need for respect. Without respect for the person in charge, a parent cannot control his children, and a manager cannot control his team.

For the sake of this discussion, I believe that there are two types of respect: respect for the person and respect for the position. Respect for you as a person comes from the strength of your personality and your skills, your accomplishments, and your abilities. Respect for the position does not come from you. It comes from inside each of your team members. In this case, it's not you that they respect, it is simply the authority invested in you as department manager.

Either type of respect—respect for you or respect for the position—will provide you with the platform to manage your department, but both types are needed for you to really succeed in your role.

～ Key Points ～

❖ Being a parent is good training for being a manager. In both, you provide praise, discipline, guidance, direction, leadership, and a pleasant environment.

❖ The first step toward being a good manager is caring about the people in your group.

❖ There are three basic types of skills required to be an effective and competent manager: interpersonal skills, business skills and good judgment.

❖ Respect is a key component of good management.

CHAPTER 2

MANAGEMENT REALITIES

∽ Congratulations, You Get to Manage Your Friends ∽

Wow, the old manager left, and they had to pick a new one. You had more experience than most of the people in the group. You also do great work, are often asked for help by less-skilled team members, and are viewed as a team leader. As a result, you were promoted, and now you are the manager. First, the good news, your pay will probably go up and your friends and family will congratulate you. Now the bad news, your co-workers will now look at you differently. The more junior people will be happy you got the job because they see that the company promotes from within, and they know they were not ready to be the manager. Yet in a year or two, these same people will hope you leave so they can be the manager.

Others in your group will be jealous and/or resentful of you because they think they should have gotten the job instead of you. They will smile at you, wish you well, say to your face that you are definitely the right person for the job, and then quietly curse you when no one is listening. Others will be happy you got the job, not because it's good for your career, but because they think it will be good for their career. In other words, they think you like them, or at least that you like them more than the old boss did. There will also be others who could care less. These people have no desire to be a manager and as long as you leave them alone, you're just a different guy in a suit who will most likely be gone in a year or two anyway.

In all cases, however, you are now the boss, and they will treat you differently. They know that their next raise, promotion, and maybe paycheck is in your hands. They will be nicer to you, let you get coffee first at the coffee machine, laugh a little louder and a little more often at your jokes, and slowly start acting more like a subordinate than a peer. You won't be asked to go out to lunch with them as often, but they will always go out to lunch with you if you ask. They will also be more guarded in what they say to you. After all, YOU can't complain about the boss anymore! In reality, you're no longer one-of-the-gang.

You will also slowly change the way you speak to them. You now have to ask/tell them to do things and expect it will be done. You also can't joke with them as much because you know (or will soon figure out) that they are now listening to the things you are saying in a different way. Among other things, they are trying to read between the lines to figure out if you are really saying what you mean.

> They best way to understand this phenomenon—the change from subordinate to manager—is to think about how you treat your boss and understand that you are now being treated by your subordinates in a similar fashion.

∼ The Management Dress Code ∼

Even though the general rules of dress apply everywhere, every company is different, so be careful to adapt this section to your specific environment. When you were an individual contributor, you were judged on how well you performed a specific task. If you were a computer programmer, it was how well you programmed. If you were a telephone salesperson, it was how much you sold. As a manager, you will be judged based on your decision-making ability; this includes ALL types of judgment, including what you wear. After all, if you don't have the common sense to wear something appropriate to work, how can you be trusted to make good business decisions?

> Remember, the other managers are now your peers. Observe how they dress. If you want to get promoted again, see how the level above them dress.

Unless you have a strong need to make a personal fashion statement, dress in a similar fashion to them. As silly as this may sound, it's true. As you will see, if you go to your boss's staff meeting wearing jeans and everyone else is in a suit and tie, you most likely will feel out of place and will not be taken as seriously.

In short, dressing appropriately will not necessarily help you, but *failing to dress appropriately* can hurt your upward mobility.

∼ Following the Company Line ∼

Rule number one. Let me say this again. Rule number one.

> Sometimes you can complain about the company to your peers, but never complain about the company to your subordinates or superiors.

Think about it: as a manager, are you going to promote someone who continually complains about the company? I think not. Now let's look at the other side of the coin. How motivated would you be if your boss was continually saying the company is lousy, doing poorly, and is badly run? You may be motivated to update your resume and find a new job, but that's about it.

Remember, you are now part of "the management." Being part of management means, among other things, supporting senior management's objectives. This means taking their vision and goals and adapting it to your department. If the company is doing something dishonest or illegal, that is something different, but just because you don't like the marketing plan or you disagree with the new vacation policy, it doesn't mean you can ignore them. It's your job to facilitate your boss's vision and success. Make no mistake—if you don't, it will affect your raise, your bonus, your upward mobility, and possibly your job.

∼ Other Managers Are Now Your Peers ∼

You know those other managers that you had to be nice to before you became a manager? Guess what? They are now your peers. Cool, huh? Now, as part of your boss's management team, you will start working with the other managers as part of a team. Your relationship with these people will quickly change. You will find that in addition to managing your department, you will now also be dealing with a whole new set of cross-department issues. Many of these cross-department issues are industry and company related, rather than task related. Here are some typical examples of the issues you will be facing.

- ❊ An employee in your department wants to move to someone else's department.
- ❊ Having to decide which department gets the new office space with a view of the ocean.
- ❊ Having to divide your boss's budget when there are limited resources for training, travel, bonuses, and other new hires.
- ❊ Having to figure out whom to lay off when your boss has been told by senior management to reduce staff by a specified number of people.

The truth is, as the newest manager on the block, expect to be on the short end of the stick unless your boss helps you out. These things take a while to figure out. If possible, use one of the other managers as a mentor to teach you the ropes. If you can't, don't beat yourself up too badly if for a while the other managers are playing the manager game better than you. After all, for you, interdepartmental politics is a new game. Know that if this year you get stuck with a bad budget because you didn't play the game well, then next year you'll learn from your mistakes.

∽ Managers Live in Fish Tanks ∽

Fish tanks? Does this sound dumb or what? This is a phenomenon that we have all seen, and the higher level the manager, the worse it gets. People watch, listen, and try to figure out the intentions of the managers above them. For example, a senior manager sees you leaving the office at 6:00 o'clock one night and says to you, "Good to see you've been working so hard." Then you spend the rest of the evening trying to figure out what she meant. Was she glad you were working late? Did she see the great analysis you did the previous week? Did your name come up in conversation as a hard worker? Did she previously think you were not working hard and now you're doing better? Was she making idle chatter, and it didn't mean a thing? Did she mean that if I continue working late and working hard that I'll be promoted? As another example, your manager seems to be spending a lot of time these days with his door shut. Is he looking for a new job? Is he working on something secret? Is he taking daily naps?

Now remember that you are a manager. Logic dictates that people are now looking at you in the same way.

∾ Key Points ∾

❀ When you first become a manager, your pay will probably go up and your friends and family will congratulate you.

❀ Once promoted, your co-workers will look at you differently. Junior co-workers will be happy you got a promotion. More senior co-workers may be jealous and/or resentful, and others could not care less.

❀ As a manager, you will be judged on your decision-making ability. This means all types of judgment, including what you wear, so always dress appropriately.

❀ Sometimes you can complain about the company to your peers, but never complain about the company to your subordinates or superiors.

❀ Now you are part of management. Being part of management means, among other things, supporting senior management's objectives.

❀ Always remember that managers live in fish tanks. (I hope you can swim.)

CHAPTER 3

MANAGING YOUR TEAM: THE GOOD STUFF

∼ Work Is Not a Democracy; It's a Dictatorship ∼

You are not only the manager of your group, you are also its leader. As a result, you certainly can, and should, get input from your staff, but the decision is yours and yours alone. You should be fair. You should be respectful of your staff members and should carefully weigh your options. That being said, you also have to make decisions based on what is best for the company, not because you like it or because it feels good, but because it's your job. This attitude is best summed up in the expression "Business is Business," and it's true. I once had to lay off a friend; he understood, but I hated it. A friend also once laid me off. Even though I agreed that her decision was the correct one, she hated to do it. In both cases, however, it was decided fairly, it was the right thing for the company, and that is what we are paid to do.

Easy decisions, like where to have the department holiday party, you can leave up to a vote. But when it comes time to make hard decisions, the decision is yours and yours alone. By the way, it's also your job to take responsibility for your decisions, both good and bad.

> As a general rule, if you try to be too nice and leave every decision to a department vote, you will be viewed as indecisive, weak, ineffective, and an obstacle to getting things done.

On the whole, however, the good news is that you get to call your department's shots. And that's cool!

～ Developing Trust ～

Trust is an essential component of teamwork and leadership. A trusted relationship between you and your subordinates is essential to your success and effectiveness as a manager. You must be able to trust them and they must be able to trust you.

Trust is an interesting thing between a subordinate and a manager. The manager has to take the lead. As the manager, you must demand honesty from your staff and make your anger known if someone lies, only tells you the good news and not the bad news, or tells half truths. In return, when one of your staff members promptly and honestly tells you about bad news and/or unpleasant issues, you must work with them constructively to solve the problem, rather than punish them for it. You will find that your constructive attitude toward their problems will help them learn to trust you.

If there is someone in your group who is untrustworthy, you would be well advised to remove them from your group when the first opportunity arises. Likewise, if they don't trust you, you're managing poorly. Find out why they don't trust you and work on it. They don't have to like you, they don't have to like working for you, but to be an effective manager you must have their trust and respect.

∽ Motivating Your Group ∽

Management in the truest sense of the word is the ability to get things done through the efforts of others. That said, as the manager, it is very important for you to understand that while it certainly is important for you to personally do a quality job, it is equally (and probably more) important that your group does good quality work.

This is a very key point for you to understand: People do their best work when they are properly motivated. The thing you have to figure out is how to motivate them.

From my perspective, motivating people has two main components: environmental and individual. Environmental motivation is best defined as the mood, sense of purpose, stability, and dynamics of the group. In other words, "Is it a nice place to work?"

Your job as manager is to establish the best environment you can for your people. Because you are part of a larger organization, you can't totally control your group's environment no matter how good of a manager you are. There are many things that you can't control, such as company mergers, bad managers at the level above you, the company's financial stability, and unreasonable goals and deadlines imposed on you by upper management. As time passes, it is inevitable that you will occasionally be placed in some or all of these difficult situations. Your ability to maintain a motivated department during tough times could very possibly be the difference between getting promoted and being laid off.

Individual motivation refers to the things that motivate a specific person. The hard thing about this one is that different things motivate different people. Some people are motivated by the chance of promotion. Some people gain motivation by being recognized. Other people are motivated by money, any one of a million other things, or sometimes nothing at all. In essence, you are helping them be successful, which in turn helps you.

> It's your job as the manager to figure out what motivates each of your team members and where appropriate, treat them in a way that motivates them.

To sum it up, first you have to create a general environment that is conducive to motivation. Second, you have to work with each team member to assure that his or her individual needs are being met. The key here is to meet each persons needs in a way that also meets your objectives and the objectives of the company.

Here is one last thing to consider. Some people are always naturally motivated and are great to have on your team. There are also people who never seem motivated and are continually a bad influence on your group. These people may be in the wrong job, they may be having some short-term personal problems, or they may just not like you (yes, YOU). In any event, sometimes you can turn these people around, and sometimes you have to remove them from your organization.

As a new manager, if you have to remove someone from your group, your best action is to discuss the issue with your boss and/or the Human Resources (HR) department as soon as possible. Not only do they have more experience in these matters than you, but also they will have to get involved in the removal process at some point anyway. That said, it's better to tell them sooner rather than later.

∼ Allowing for Employee's Personal Needs ∼

There is an old expression that says, "People should work-to-live not live-to-work." Accordingly, upon occasion and within certain bounds, you should allow an employee's personal life to take precedent over their job. I don't mean you should let someone come in late every morning because they like to hit the nightclubs until 2:00 a.m. every night with their buddies. I mean that if you have a good employee who is working through a difficult personal or health issue, you should help him or her out. Not only is this the right thing to do as a human being, but also it will almost always build incredible loyalty to both you and the company. In the long run, this loyalty is good for everyone.

Over the years, I have occasionally had members in my team ask for help. One person asked if she could take two-hour lunches for a couple of months until she could find long-term day care for her elderly mother. She said that she would make up the time by coming in early. Not only did she come in early every day, she often stayed late just to make sure that all her work was completed. Another employee and his wife were having trouble conceiving a child. With the help of their doctor, a number of tests were scheduled. This affected work because he would be coming in late once or twice a week for two months. He also promised to make up the time, which he did. I didn't keep a close watch of his coming and going because I trusted him. But, best I could guess, he worked about two hours for every one hour he was out. The best news in this story is that he and his wife had a healthy baby boy. Please note: Let me say that again, please note, before you grant special help to a member of your team, talk to your manager and HR to make sure that you are doing it correctly and in a way that is consistent with company policy. HR people deal with this stuff all the time. They may even come up with ideas that you and/or the employee didn't consider.

When you do nice things to help your team members, there are three extra benefits. On the personal side, it feels good to be able to help someone. Secondly, people talk. The other members of your team will know what you did and that will increase their loyalty to you. Lastly, when you need that person's help because of a tight deadline or because of a project you underestimated, they will be there for you, which is good for you and good for the company.

As they say, "No good turn goes unpunished" (I don't know who "they" are, but it seems that they say a lot of stuff). There is one down side to helping people in this way. As each of these issues arises, you have to make sure that they are truly one-of-a-kind exceptions and that you are not setting department or company precedence.

You don't want to be seen as playing favorites or bending company rules for specific individuals. The last thing you want to hear from another employee is "Why won't you do this for me, you did it for Larry?" If asked this question, you will have to answer it honestly and with valid reasoning.

∼ Building Loyalty ∼

Here I go with the old expressions again. There is an old expression that says, "To have a good friend, you have to be a good friend." I believe that loyalty follows the same paradigm. You have to let them take credit for their accomplishments. You have to protect them when problems and/or bad politics arise. You have to go to bat for them when they need it. You have to be a good mentor, a good teacher, and a good listener. In essence, loyalty is a product of good leadership.

> If you want your people to be loyal to you, you have to be loyal to them.

I believe that trust is a key ingredient of loyalty. As a result, I demand honesty from the people in my group. If I can't trust them, I can't work with them. If I can't work with them, then I won't have them on my team. In return, however, I am very loyal to my people.

∾ The Better the Employee, the More Flexible the Rules ∾

This is a phenomenon you should know about. It's not a hard-and-fast rule or a standard company policy; it's more just general human nature. It has been my observation over the years (Wow, did I say over the years? Boy do I feel old) that the harder someone works, the better job they do, and/or the more likable they are, the more management is willing to help them. Also, little things like a cubicle near a window, slightly altered work hours, paying for the home Internet connection to work from home, and similar stuff (stuff being the technical term for little niceties) seems to come their way. These are also the people who tend to get bigger pay raises, larger bonuses, better project assignments, and more promotions. Over time you will find yourself giving these types of things to your best people. The lesson for you in this story is that these rules also apply to you. If you work hard, do a good job, and get along well with your bosses, you too can be on the receiving side of these niceties.

∼ The Rule of "No Surprises" ∼

I have said many times that if it's not my birthday, surprises are usually a bad thing. A co-worker of mine liked to say that bad news doesn't get better with time. These two sayings ring very true in the business arena. When there is an issue within your department, the worst thing you can do is not tell your boss. This may sound counterintuitive, but it is the best possible course of action. There are four main reasons (and lots of little reasons) why you want to tell your boss about your department's problems. First, when you tell your boss about a problem and propose a solution (always have a proposed solution), it lets your boss know that you realize a problem exists and you are thinking of ways to solve it.

All departments have problems. That's why departments need managers. If your boss sees that your department's problems are being addressed, it will help raise your boss's confidence in your management ability. Second, when you tell your boss that a project is going well, he will believe you. This is because he knows that you also tell him when issues arise. Third, your boss has the right to know—it's his group. Also, if he found out about an issue in your department from others, it will put you in a very bad situation. You will either look like you don't know what is going on in your own department, or that you know and don't want to tell your boss. Fourth, once the problem is fixed, you can take credit for it and add it to the accomplishments section of your annual performance report. Also, if needed at a future time, you can also put it on your resume.

Anyway, back to discussing "no surprises." As a general rule, good companies can solve or at least mitigate most business problems if they have enough time to react. By telling your boss early about an issue, you can help keep the problem small (which will make your life a lot more pleasant since you are the department manager). Also, it lets your boss know that you are paying attention and being proactive, rather than reactive.

Now, here is the definition of a big problem. Are you ready? OK, here it comes. A big problem is when your boss's boss is mad because of something that went wrong in your department. This is very career limiting. If your boss's boss doesn't like you, you will never get another promotion.

Let's talk about one more thing on the surprise front. I would bet money that your boss doesn't like to be surprised by his boss. I would also bet money (I don't actually gamble, but I like the expression) that when your boss is asked, "How are things going?" he would like to be able to give a fact-based quality answer. I would bet even more money that you would like your boss's answer to be the following: "Things are going well. There's an issue with a person in Joe's department, but Joe has come up with a great solution. I'm confident he can handle it. He's really turning into a good solid manager." See, I said you would like it. By the way, I assume you know that you were Joe.

Now let's turn the situation around. There is still an issue with a person in your department, and your name is still Joe. However, you didn't tell your boss about the issue. But, your boss's boss knows. Now, when your boss is asked, "How are things going?" he says things are going great. His boss then says, "What about the problem with that guy who works for Joe?" Surprise!!! My bet is that your boss won't be pleased that he didn't know about the issue ahead of time.

~ Key Points ~

❀ You are not only the manager of your group; you are also its leader.

❀ You should always make decisions based on what is best for the company, not because you like it or because it feels good, but because it's your job.

❀ A trusted relationship between you and your subordinates is essential to your success and effectiveness as a manager.

❀ You must be able to trust them, and they must be able to trust you.

❀ If there is someone in your group who is untrustworthy, you would be well advised to remove them from your group when the opportunity arises.

❀ People do their best work when they are properly motivated. The thing you have to figure out is how to motivate them.

❀ Your job as manager is to establish the best environment you can for your people.

❀ If you have to remove someone from your group, your best action is to discuss the issue with your boss and/or Human Resources as soon as possible.

❀ If you have a good employee who is working through a difficult personal or health issue, you should help him or her out. Not only is this the right thing to do, but also it will almost always build incredible loyalty to both you and the company.

❀ If you want your people to be loyal to you, you have to be loyal to them.

❀ The harder someone works, the better job they do, and/or the more likable they are, the more management is willing to help them.

❀ When there is an issue within your department, the worst thing you can do is not tell your boss. This may sound counterintuitive, but it is the best possible course of action. But also always try to propose an effective solution.

CHAPTER 4

MANAGING YOUR TEAM: THE BAD STUFF

∾ Making Promises You Can't Keep ∾

There is an old expression that says, "No good deed goes unpunished." When trying to motivate a subordinate, hire a new employee, make someone a project leader, or get a salary adjustment for an underpaid staff member, you can promise to try, but never promise to deliver. If you promise something to a subordinate and then can't deliver, you will lose credibility with that staff member and potentially your whole staff. Additionally, if he goes to HR, you may find yourself in trouble. Remember, as his boss, you are a representative of the company. If you promise someone a raise, extra vacation time, or anything else, your company may have to comply, which means your management and the HR department will most likely be very upset with you. At best, people will be angry; at worst, you may lose your job.

Here is another example of a "promise gone bad" (sounds like an episode of the *Jerry Springer Show*). You promise to hire someone, and that person quits their old job just as you realize that your boss stopped all hiring a week ago. This poor guy is out of work because of you. He may simply yell and scream at you, your boss, HR, and anyone else who will listen, or he may sue the company. In any case, you have caused major problems for the person you were trying to hire and have made yourself look totally incompetent as a manager.

(As an aside, in your own career, never quit your old job until you have an offer in writing for your new job.)

There are some specific times when you can promise things to the people in your group. The key is to get permission ahead of time from HR and your boss, and get it in writing or at least in an internal email. For example, it may be a company policy to promote a computer programmer to a senior computer programmer if she passes a specific Microsoft certification program. In that case (again after speaking with HR first), you can promise the programmer that you will promote her if she passes the certification.

∼ How to Discipline a Staff Member ∼

There are many different types of discipline (evil laugh goes here). No seriously, there are many types of discipline. Like a parent disciplining a child, the punishment has to match the crime.

> You can't fire someone just because you want to. You do, however, have to act decisively if someone does something dangerous, illegal, or totally contrary to company policy.

The simplest and best form of discipline is constructive criticism. It has been my experience that sometimes you have a good employee doing the wrong thing. It may be due to a lack of skill in a particular area, or it may be a lack of understanding of the rules. In either case, it's your job as the manager to pull the person aside and explain what he is doing wrong and what is needed to improve/correct the situation. When I give constructive criticism, I usually start by talking about something the person is doing well. I then say that although he is generally doing good work, he needs a little help in one particular area. I talk about the issue in a friendly, mentoring manner. Once I get my point across, I like to change the subject to something fun and non-work-oriented, like the Red Sox (yes, I'm a Sox fan), weekend plans, or the next company picnic. This change of subject is designed to end the conversation on a good note, leaving the employee feeling good that he learned something new rather than feeling that he was doing something wrong. You also want to leave him feeling that the boss (yes, you) is still very supportive of him as a person and as an employee.

For discipline stronger than constructive criticism, begin by giving HR and your boss a heads-up. All HR departments have (or should have) a predefined process to warn, discipline, and, if needed, fire an employee. The steps in this process should be designed to meet legal requirements, treat the individual with respect and dignity, protect the company, and protect you as their manager. Follow these rules exactly as HR requires.

∼ The Seven Types of Difficult Employees ∼

Let's say it like it is. Managing difficult employees stinks. It wastes lots of time, takes lots of energy, tends to cause problems, usually creates lots of paperwork, and just isn't any fun. Now for the good news; well sorry, there is no good news. The best news I can give you is that if you handle the situation correctly you may be able to dramatically improve their attitude, work quality, and general performance. On the other hand, if the person doesn't or can't improve, and if he doesn't leave on his own, you can eventually remove him (of course, with the help of HR).

> The truth is, as funny as it sounds, the best way to deal with a bad employee is to not hire him in the first place. That's why the hiring process is so important.

With all that said, let's discuss what to do if you do have a difficult person on your team. To begin, there are several different kinds of difficult employees. I like to categorize them as Sleazy, Grumpy, Lazy, Brainy, Tardy, Dummy, and Troubled (yeah, I know, but this was more fun then categorizing them as types one to seven).

Next, I'll describe these types of employees and the appropriate action for each one. Please note that the first five types are honesty- and/or motivation-based, while the last two could be you or I at any given time.

∼ Sleazy ∼

This type of person is marginally honest. He does not do anything blatantly illegal or clearly against company policy, but pushes the limits with no particular regard for the company, his fellow employees, or your customers. Classic "sleazy" examples include: padding his expense account, selling inappropriate products to customers, stealing customers and leads from other salespeople, taking credit for other people's work, and doing things that other employees find repugnant.

Generally speaking, I don't trust this kind of person. My advice to you is not to trust them either and be pleasantly surprised if you find them to be honest. Your best plan of action to straighten them out is to talk to your HR person first, then sit down with the employee (maybe with HR) and lay out the law in writing. For example, if they've been selling inappropriate products to your customers, say that you will be monitoring their sales, and, if the practice continues, they will be reassigned or asked to leave the company.

> You have to be tough and make it plain to your group that questionable business practices are not acceptable.

∾ Grumpy ∾

Well, we all know grumpy people. You see it in their facial expressions, their speech, their body language, and their general attitude. There are a number of reasons why people are grumpy at work: some are personality-related, some are non-work-related, and some are work-related. From a personality perspective, these people are few and far between, but some people are grumpy by nature and that is just how they are. You have to learn to manage around it, or over time, move them out of your department. Regarding non-work-related grumpiness, I classify this as a troubled person and will discuss them later in this section. Work-related grumpiness can very often be corrected through good management (yes, your good management).

Very often people are grumpy at work for a specific reason. These reasons include low pay, lack of challenging work, lack of training, lack of visibility to upper management, no perceived chance of advancement, and other similar issues. Your job as the person's manager is to work with the employee to define the specific issue or issues causing their unhappiness and define a plan to correct it. I have seen many peoples' attitudes improve dramatically when the proper steps are taken to address their concerns.

∾ Lazy ∾

This is the *"I'm going to do as little as possible to still keep my job"* guy. On a personal note, I'm a very hard worker, so lazy people drive me crazy. I personally have no tolerance for laziness, so I tend to continually be on these people to get their job done. That way, you can easily monitor their performance in an analytical fashion. This approach allows you to objectively evaluate their output and take appropriate positive and negative actions as needed.

> It's my opinion that the best way to handle lazy people is to give them tasks that can be specifically measured in regard to quality and quantity.

∾ Brainy ∾

Smart is a good thing. By brainy, I mean a "know-it-all." These people are typically hard-working, smart, and do a good job. The problem is that they drive their peers crazy and cause tension within the department. This problem can generally be fixed by occasionally having an honest discussion with the person over a cup of coffee. Basically, ask him to quiet down a little and treat his fellow employees with a little more tolerance and respect.

∾ Tardy ∾

On occasion, everyone comes in late, has a long lunch, or leaves early. But every so often, someone abuses the privilege. They always come in fifteen or twenty minutes late, and/or they always take two-hour lunches, and/or they are always out the door early. Not only are you not getting your money's worth from this person, but also their lack of respect for the company's schedule can have a very disruptive effect on the rest of your team, particularly if your other team members are working long hours. I generally try to correct this problem by first having a friendly discussion with the person and telling him that his actions are unacceptable and to work the required hours. If his schedule doesn't improve, then work with HR to write a formal reprimand. This reprimand should include the specific actions to be stopped and the consequences if their actions continue. Generally, you will find that HR is very skilled in writing these types of letters.

∾ Dummy ∾

The dummy category falls into two types: those who don't have the proper training to do the job and those who don't have the ability to do the job. For those who need additional training, the answer is obvious—get them some training. For those who don't have the ability, the right thing to do is to have a heart-to-heart talk with him and help him find a different position within the company that better fits his skills and abilities.

∾ Troubled ∾

Treat this person with tenderness, respect, support, and assistance. Virtually everyone has times in their life when they are overtaken by deep personal issues like severe illness, the death of a loved one, a divorce, financial difficulties, personal heath issues, or other similar crises. These events can seemingly overnight make your best employees unproductive, detached, or a little self-destructive. As their manager, you are in a position to give them support and guidance, direct them toward special company resources, and generally make their life a little easier (for a short time) until they are able to deal with the personal issues at hand. It's not only the right thing to do as their employer, it's the right thing to do as a human being.

∼ Key Points ∼

❀ If you promise something to a subordinate and then can't deliver, you will lose credibility with that staff member and potentially your whole staff.

❀ The simplest and best form of office discipline is constructive criticism.

❀ For discipline stronger than constructive criticism, begin by giving HR and your boss a heads-up. All HR departments have (or should have) a predefined process to warn, discipline, and, if needed, fire an employee.

❀ Don't forget the seven kinds of difficult employees: Sleazy, Grumpy, Lazy, Brainy, Tardy, Dummy, and Troubled. (Memorize this list, and you can impress your friends at parties.)

CHAPTER 5

NAVIGATING OFFICE POLITICS

∽ Being the Chief Cheerleader for Your Department ∽

As the department manager, you should be the number one advocate for your group. It's your responsibility to assure that your department has the resources it needs to function properly, receives the appropriate respect from other parts of the company, performs its functions effectively, and gets the recognition that both you and your people deserve.

> The main way the company will know how well your department is doing is by you telling anyone who will listen.

It will benefit you personally if your team is perceived as important to the company. Now here comes the cheerleader part. I don't mean be obnoxious about it; just say it in small, appropriate doses. For example, when asked casual questions by senior people in the company such as "How's it going?" don't say, "Great, how about you?" Instead, say, "Things are going really well. For the fifth month in a row my department is 20 percent above our quota." Have four or five of these informational nuggets at the ready. These quick, informational exchanges can give your department a big boost at unexpected times. For example, the senior executive whom you told about your quota in the last example may need a regional manger somewhere, or at the next corporate meeting that executive may use your department as an example of teams that are exceeding their quota.

You should also be the chief cheerleader for the individuals in your group. This builds loyalty in the group toward you, and it gives the individuals in your team the recognition they deserve. For example, when your boss asks, "How's it going?" you can say, "Great, in fact Joe just negotiated a great service agreement with one of our vendors." This type of answer to your boss, or other executive, tells him three things. First, and the most obvious, is that Joe is doing a great job. Second, is that you are the kind of manager who is willing to give deserved credit to the individual members of your team. Third, good things are happening within your department, and you are smart enough to recognize it.

As chief cheerleader, you should also be showing interest, excitement, and enthusiasm in your department's role within the company, the work your group is doing, and how your group is performing. This differs from my previous advice because here you are explaining your department's importance to the company, rather than just your department's accomplishments. For example, you might say, "I'm excited that the new technology we developed in the systems department helped the sales department get our products into Wal-Mart." This statement says two things at once: We are doing our job well, and we provide real value to the company. This show of enthusiasm will raise the energy level of the people around you, including your team, your peers, and, to a certain extent, your boss.

There is one last role for you as chief cheerleader, and that's to cheer for yourself. It's good to be selfless and pass credit on to your group members; it's also very advantageous to be your own chief cheerleader in a humble kind of way. You don't want to say how great you are, because people will just roll their eyes at you. Instead, learn to talk about your successes and accomplishments in a factual and matter of fact way. You can get your point across without feeling like you're boasting.

∼ Manager-Level Politics ∼

In the introductory chapter of this book, I alluded to the fact that management-level politics are very different from individual-contributor politics. As an individual contributor, you can generally stay clear of office politics all together if you wish. You can just keep your head down and do your work. Politics at the individual contributor level tend to be related to who gets the best office (or cube), who learns the newest technology, who gets the best projects, and who doesn't get their sales region cut. Simply said, all the individual-level politics are about you and your stuff.

> Moving from being an individual contributor to manager is like moving from being single to being married.

Now, it's not all about you. It's still a little about you, but mostly, it is now about us, you and the team, you and the spouse. As a manager, your ability to play the game not only affects you, but it also affects the people in your department.

As a manager, your politics are still primarily with your peers, but now your peers are the other managers. You'll find that your new peer group is much better at politics than the individual contributors you used to compete with. That is how and why they became managers. You'll also find that you will still be fighting for some of the same things like office space, projects, sales territory, and the like, but they will be at the department level, rather than on an individual basis.

You may also find that some politics go away. For example, in the business analysis group, politics at the individual-contributor level revolve around who gets what project. As the manager of that department, by default, you get all the business analysis projects because you head the group. You then decide which analyst works on which task. Now, if your department's role is clearly defined within the company, there are also no turf wars. Any project turf wars for specific projects are now under you. It is your staff who will be fighting to get the best projects.

Office politics with your peers is like sports. You can't win them all. Sometimes you win and sometimes you lose. In either case, learn from what you did right and wrong, and also learn from what your peers did right and wrong. By understanding and observing office politics, you really can learn from (and take advantage of) the mistakes of others.

∽ Managing Up ∽

Managing up is one of the most important things you must learn to do. To a large extent, the levels of management above you control your success and future at the company. If they like you, respect you, and think you can help their careers, they will increase your responsibility, promote you, raise your pay, and generally make your work life more pleasant.

> Keep in mind, managing up effectively does not mean kissing someone's backside, sucking up, brown nosing, or whatever other cliché you would like to use.

Effectively managing up is about communication, trust, standing your ground when needed, producing quality work, and being responsive to all levels of management. If your boss needs a report by Friday, get it to him on Friday, or Thursday if you can. If you need additional resources, do your homework and clearly explain why you need it, how much it will cost, and its return on investment to the company (e.g., better analysis, faster service, cost savings, etc.)

Managing up is also the art of using your boss to help you get things done. Generally speaking, if you have good ideas that your boss likes, he will help you, if it is within his means to do so. After all, when you and your department do good things, it not only looks good for you, it looks good for your boss.

The next place managing up is important is when there are problems. The general rule is that whenever you tell your boss about a problem, also have one or more potential solutions. That said, it's also OK to ask your boss for advice on how to handle a particular situation. After all, he has more experience than you and may come up with some really good ideas. So seek his advice and learn.

> A good manager is also a good teacher and mentor.

A strong relationship with your boss will not only help you get the resources and recognition you desire, it also will have a profound effect on the relationship and influence you have with your peer managers. If you have a good relationship with your boss, particularly if it is better than the relationship your boss has with your peers, it puts you in a powerful position when dealing with your fellow managers.

(Hmm, should I use a New England based expression that some people may not have heard to describe the following very important topic? Yeah, what the heck!) OK, here it goes: The next topic is wicked important.

You can only effectively fight battles at your management level.

If you try to gain the advantage over someone at your boss's level, you will lose. Even worse, a company re-organization in the future could have you reporting to the person with whom you were fighting. If that happens, then to use another New England based expression, you're toast (that's a bad thing). If you have to fight a battle with a person at your boss's level, let your boss do it. In all seriousness, I cannot stress enough how important it is for you to learn this lesson.

Lastly, take great comfort in knowing that your boss is on your side. If he is the one who promoted you or hired you into the position, he will want you to succeed. After all, it was his decision that gave you your new job in the first place. As a result, your performance (good or bad) reflects on his decision-making ability.

∾ **Managing Down** ∾

In a manner of speaking, most of this book is about managing down. As a result, the only thing I will say here is to remember to communicate with your subordinates in an honest, constructive, and consistent manner.

> Remember at all times that your success as a manager is in large part based on the success of the people under you.

There is one more thing I would like say here. In many ways, managing down is like managing up, except you are the recipient instead of the provider. Foster an environment within your department that allows your people to "manage up" to you. Just as your boss will take advantage of the information you provide him, you can take advantage of the information passed your way when your team is managing up to you.

Well, I guess I have yet one more thing to say. During times of company uncertainty, due to mergers, buyouts, bad sales, and other company issues, remember to manage down often. More correctly stated, like you, your team members may be worried about layoffs, budget cuts, plant closings, office consolidations, and other scary things. Talk to your team about the issues often and honestly. Tell them what you know (to the extent that company policy allows) and tell them what you don't know. When times are uncertain, communication to your group is essential. Also, as their manager, it will also be of great benefit to you and the company.

> Honest and open communicating during difficult times will be of great comfort to your team.

∼ Managing Across ∼

Ah yes, this is where the fun begins. Rule number one is to be a team player. It will make it easier for you, easier for your boss, and easier for your group.

Assuming that your peers are also managers, your boss is then a manager of managers. As a result, his job is very different from yours. Whereas your job is to assure that specific hands-on work is being appropriately performed, your boss's job is to assemble a cohesive management team that works together as a unit for the greater good of the organization. Your boss wants a team that works together.

> Unless you are very, very good or unless you are best friends with your boss, if you are not a team player, you will eventually be pushed out of the organization.

Also, if your peers can't or won't work with you, they can make your life miserable. Also, never forget about reorganizations. If your boss leaves or is promoted, there is a large probability that you may find yourself working for one of your current peers. Now, guess what? If you treated that person poorly when he was your peer, chances are he will be very unpleasant to you as your manager.

Another thing to keep in mind—helping your peers also helps your boss. As he wants you and your department to be successful, he also wants his other managers and their departments to be successful.

OK, now that we have all the good stuff on the table, I am sad to say that working with your peers is not always a bed of roses. Depending on your company's culture and/or your specific job function, you may find yourself continually competing with your peers for resources, budget dollars, control of specific business areas, bonus dollars, stock options, and a million other things. Learn the rules of the game. Don't take advantage of your peers (too much), but in the same breath, don't be a pushover and let them take advantage of you either. You will find that many of the rules you learned in elementary school still apply. If you let them take your lunch money today without a fight, they will probably try to take it again tomorrow.

∽ Knowing What Not to Send in an Email ∽

Here is the rule. Don't put anything in an email that you wouldn't want your boss, husband, wife, kids, staff, mother, peers, customers, and the rest of the world to read. Your emails can easily be forwarded to other people inside and outside the company without your knowledge. This could have very unpleasant ramifications. The same rule also applies to voice mail.

I strongly suggest that you do not do any of the following, but if you find the need to tell someone something mean, bad, unprofessional, or just plain obnoxious, either do it in person or over the phone on an unrecorded line. That way, you can deny it later. You really don't want stuff like that permanently documented and/or passed around the office like a bad joke. It could cost you your job and/or your reputation, and based on the subject matter, it could also be a basis for a legal action against you.

I'd like to share an email story with you—one that I strongly suggest you don't try. When email first gained popularity, a friend of mine loved to trade email-based jokes with his friends. You know, jokes about politics, jokes related to current events, and various types of, well, let's say, off-color jokes. He accidentally copied a fellow employee on an email he was sending to a friend. Upon investigation by the company, they found hundreds of non-business-related emails in his company email. He almost lost his job.

The moral of the story is that your work email is for work. If you want to send jokes to your friends, do it on your time and from your personal email. These days, companies have very strict policies on email use. That said, no matter how good of an employee you are, if they catch you sending and receiving inappropriate emails, you could lose your job. This is particularly likely now that you are a manager. The reason is that if you accidentally send a sexual, racial, or just plain gross or nasty email to a subordinate, you are opening up the company to lawsuits. Guess how the company will protect itself? You got it—they will say that one bad employee caused the problem and then walk you to the door.

I have one last item for you regarding email. Many companies, based on the type of product or service they provide, may be required to save all emails for up to seven years. For example, financial services companies are required to save emails for three years or seven years based on the specific type of service being provided. This means that just because you delete an email from a work email account, don't assume it's actually gone. Even though you can't see it anymore, the company can.

∾ Key Points ∾

❀ As the department manager, you should be the number one advocate for your group.

❀ Be the chief cheerleader for the individuals in your group. This builds loyalty in the group toward you, and it gives the individuals in your team the recognition they deserve.

❀ Moving from being an individual contributor to manager is like moving from being single to being married. Now, it's not all about you.

❀ As a manager, your politics are still primarily with your peers, but now your peers are the other managers who are much better at politics than the individual contributors with whom you used to compete.

❀ Managing up is one of the most important things you must learn to do. To a large extent, the levels of management above you control your success and future at the company.

❀ Effectively managing up is about communication, trust, standing your ground, producing quality work, and being responsive to all levels of management.

❀ A strong relationship with your boss will help you get the resources and recognition you desire. It will also have a profound effect on the relationship and influence you have with your peer managers.

❀ Managing down is all about communicating with your subordinates in an honest, constructive, and consistent manner.

❀ When dealing with your peer managers be a team player. It will make it easier for you, easier for your boss, and easier for your group.

❀ Helping your peers also helps your boss.

❀ Don't put anything in an email that you wouldn't want your boss, wife, kids, staff, mother, peers, customers, and the rest of world to read.

CHAPTER 6

THE HIRING PROCESS

∽ What You Should Know ∽

For a manager, the hiring process is the combination of defining the job, getting permission to hire, working with a recruiter to find people to interview, interviewing the people, deciding which one you like, and offering him/her a job. Sounds easy, doesn't it? Well, sometimes it is easy. But more often than not, every step presents roadblocks that must be overcome.

Let's discuss each of these steps. Remember, when reading about these steps, I will always be describing it from the manager's perspective. Each of these steps also provides various challenges and frustrations for the HR generalists and recruiters, issues that are outside the scope of this book. That said, very often the most frustrating part of the process for the HR people is you. Yes YOU, the manager.

There is one very important thing to know about the hiring process, there are many laws and regulations. There are things you can and cannot say. There are things you can and cannot ask. Like you, I'm a manager not an HR person. As a result, I suggest you have a talk with your HR person to make sure you have a general understanding about the laws associated with hiring. If you accidentally say or do something really stupid, you can lose your job and/or be sued.

Probably the best piece of advice I can give you about the HR-related sections of this book, such as the hiring process, is to look beyond these pages for further information. Entire books cover the individual topics of how to interview, how to read resumes, understanding hiring laws and regulations, and so no. My hope here is to teach you how to work with HR as a manager, not to be an HR professional.

∼ In Office Lingo, It's a "Req" ∼

In office lingo, a job opening is very often called an "open requisition," abbreviated to "open req." If the req is in the budget, but not yet open, it is a "budgeted req." If the req is open, and you lose the authority to hire due to a hiring freeze or other issue, the req is referred to as becoming "closed."

∽ Getting Permission to Hire ∽

The process of getting permission to hire (yes, it's a process) is greatly affected by the nature of the hire, the current profitability of the company, your department's function within the company, and if your boss likes you and/or owes you a favor.

The process begins by writing a job description. This description specifies the job's title, salary, job duties, eligibility requirements, and other similar information. Your HR department should be able to provide you with a few examples. This job description has a number of uses (which is good considering it's a pain to write). First, it makes you sit down and think about the kind of person you want to hire and the specific duties that need to be performed. Second, your boss and/or HR will most likely require a written job description before you are allowed to open the req. Third, once open, the HR department will use the information contained in the job description to advertise the job and screen incoming applicants.

Now, here are the rules and tricks of the trade when it comes to reqs.

- ❁ As soon as a req opens, work day and night to fill it before it closes.
- ❁ Never hire someone just to get the req filled, you'll soon regret it; wait for the right person.
- ❁ Reqs that are in the budget are easier to open than reqs that are not in the budget, so pay attention during budgeting season.
- ❁ Reqs that replace a person who left (replacement reqs) are the easiest to get approved.
- ❁ A company, no mater how large or successful, can only hire a certain number of people. Very often, success in getting your req open is based on the combination of need and your ability to play company politics.

∽ Finding People to Interview ∽

Well done—your req is open. Now, the fun begins. There are various ways to find people to interview. These ways include internal transfers, employee referrals, Internet job sites, the newspaper want ads, and contingency recruiters (also referred to as headhunters). The good news is that you don't have to worry about finding people because the HR department will help you find candidates. Your job, as the hiring manager in this process, is to be very supportive and helpful to the HR department. In other words, help them help you. This happens because you are so busy with department work that you don't have the time to hire more people to help. Find the time. Let me say that again. Find the time.

> A big mistake that many managers make (including me upon occasion) is ignoring HR.

∾ Reviewing Resumes ∾

Wow, the HR person has actually collected some interesting resumes to review. Now it's your turn. Everyone has their own way of reviewing resumes. As you gain experience, you will also develop a personal method. Until you develop your own resume screening method, here is a process you can follow. When reviewing this process, understand that your goal is to try to get a mental image of the person.

- Start by reviewing their education. If they went to a high quality college, you know that most likely they're naturally bright. If they didn't attend a top school, it doesn't tell you anything. Some of the smartest, most successful people I know did not go to the top schools. It may simply mean that their parents could not afford it.
- Look at the year the person graduated college. This will give you an idea about their age. Knowing their age helps you construct your mental image of the person. Don't use their age as a selection criterion, that's illegal; use it strictly as a way to better understand the person whose resume you are reviewing.
- Look for professional certifications. Generally speaking, there are two types of certifications, those that are required by law (or regulation) to perform specified tasks and those that show proficiency in a specified area. These certifications do not necessarily guarantee proficiency, but they do show initiative. Even if they have certifications, if the position requires specific skills, test them on it.
- Review their professional experience from oldest to newest. This will give you an idea of the progression of their career.
- Take a second look at their professional experience and see how long the person spent at each company. Unless she was a consultant, if she hasn't stayed at any one company for more than a year, she will probably not stay with you long term.

I have another suggestion for you regarding reading resumes. You will be surprised how much you can learn about someone when you know how to read his or her resume properly.

When you review your first batch of resumes, review them with your manager or mentor and ask them their thoughts on each person.

∽ When You Recognize a Name on a Resume ∽

When I graduated college and started my first professional job, my first manager told me that after a while it would seem like there are only five hundred technology people working in New England, and that they just cycle from company to company. Being the worldly twenty-two-year-old that I was (please note the sarcasm), I had no idea what he was talking about and thought he was crazy. Well, he was right. Over time, if you stay in the same geographic area and the same general industry long enough, you get to know most of the companies in your industry and many of the people in those companies.

As a result, when you're looking at someone's resume, you may realize that you know the person. Alternatively, you may not know the person directly, but you may know people who worked at the same company at the same time. Use this to your advantage and consider the following:

❁ First and foremost, respect the person's privacy. Her current employer, friends, and/or spouse may not know she is looking for a new job. It's not your place to tell anyone unrelated to the hiring process.

❁ If you don't think you can work well with the person, throw their resume in the trash and move to the next one.

❁ If you really like the person, but he can't do the job, throw his resume in the trash and move on.

❁ If you are familiar with the company where the person currently works, you may be able to get a gut feel for the person's professional experience. As an example, some companies have state-of-the-art equipment and other companies do everything manually. If you're looking for a person with high-tech experience, you most likely will not find her at a low-tech-oriented firm.

❁ If you, the interviewer, know someone who has worked with the candidate (the person whose resume you are looking at), you may be tempted to call your connection and ask about the individual. If you choose to do this, don't (*don't, don't, don't*) call people at their current place of employment. You don't know the company's internal politics, and you may really be hurting the person.

❖ Should you decide to call a friend at a company where the candidate formerly worked, make sure that your friend knows that it's a confidential conversation.

∼ The Interview Process ∼

If you think you were nervous when you had an interview as an applicant, just wait until you have to do the interviewing. Until you get the hang of interviewing people, you will be as nervous as they are.

Many people say that in a thirty-minute interview, they decide in the first five minutes if they like or don't like the candidate. The remaining time is then spent either selling the candidate on the job if they like the candidate, or making small talk and re-evaluating the candidate to make sure that they are not the right person. As for me, I can't give away all my secrets, because I may be interviewing you for a job one day, but here are some tips.

When conducting an interview, it's advantageous to proceed in an organized manner. Over time, you will develop your own interview style, but in the meantime, try the following interview outline. Think of this outline as a guideline rather than a hard-and-fast rule.

- ❀ Start with a small-talk-type question or statement. This type of question/statement is designed to get the conversation started in an easy non-threatening way. For example, **"Would you like a cup of coffee?" "Did you have any trouble finding our offices?"** or **"I can't believe it's going to rain again this weekend."**

- ❀ Next, ask, **"How did you hear about the job opening?"** This question should also be easy for the candidate to answer. It gives you valuable information about the candidate such as how motivated he is to find a new job, how organized he is in his job search, and if he was internally referred by another employee. Note that if he was internally referred, not only is that a positive reference (no one likes to refer a "bad" person), but it also gives you the opportunity to discuss the candidate further with the person giving the reference.

- ❀ Next, ask them, **"Do you have a good understanding about the job that is open?"** This question allows the candidate an opportunity to learn more about the job from the manager's point of view (that would be you). If, as a result, the candidate is no longer interested, the interview ends. If the candidate is

still interested, then it is a good basis for your next question
about her previous job experience.

❖ Next, say, **"Please talk me through your resume."** If they don't
have a resume, then say, **"Please tell me about your work
experience beginning with your first real job."** This allows
the candidate to talk you through their work experience. This
should give you a good sense of their background, including
such things as why they left their previous employer, the type
of work they like doing, their ability to articulate what they
have done, and the experiences they've had that are applicable
to your job opening.

❖ Next, ask, **"Do you have any questions that I can answer for
you about the job or the company?"** This gives them a chance
to ask you questions. Not only will this help provide them
information about you (their potential new manager), the job,
and the company, but it will also give you additional information about them based on the questions they ask.

❖ Lastly, tell them about the next steps in the job process, including when they will hear back from you or your company. This
gives the candidate a sense of timing and what to expect. It's
also a nice way to signal that the interview is about to end.

In addition to the questions listed above, there are a million other
things you can ask based on the job and/or your interview style. For
example, if you need to understand their ability in a specific skill, you
can ask them a list of questions about that skill.

Some people also ask what activities the candidate does outside the
office. This gives people a chance to talk about their bowling league,
their kids, their civic activities, their golf game, and other things that are
important to them as a person. This also gives you a good sense for the
person outside the resume.

Occasionally people have fun/dumb questions that they like to ask job
candidates. I don't recommend this. As an example, here is a dumb question I was once asked when interviewing for a job: "If you could be any
kind of animal in the world, what would you be?" After thinking that the
interviewer was an idiot, I said, "I would be an eagle. It's at the top of the

food chain, and I could fly for free." He told me he liked my answer but that technically an "eagle is a bird, not an animal." Yeah, right.

Here is a list of some tried-and-true interview questions. Note that these aren't questions that I made up. People have been using them for years.

- What are your three biggest strengths and three main weaknesses?
- Why do you want to leave your current job?
- What do you think of your last employer?
- Where do you see yourself in five years?
- How would you describe yourself?
- Do you consider yourself to be a leader?
- What is your ideal job?
- How would your old manager describe you?
- What motivates you? Please give me an example.
- Do you do well under pressure? Please give me an example.
- Why should I hire you?
- Why do you want to work at our company?
- Are you a team player?
- What do you know about our company?
- Did you look at our company's website?
- What do you think of your last manager?
- What was your biggest success, personally or professionally?
- What was your biggest failure, personally or professionally?

It's well worth your time to read a book or take a seminar specializing in interview techniques.

It's important that you become a good interviewer.

❧ Deciding which Person to Hire ❧

OK, now what? You've sifted through thirty or forty resumes, orchestrated first interviews for five people, and brought two people back for second interviews. How do you decide whom to pick? Below are two small lists. One list describes things you should do and one list describes things you shouldn't do.

The things you should do.

❀ Get advice and input from the other people who interviewed the candidates. Even after years of interviewing and hiring people, I still find other people's points of view about a candidate very valuable.

❀ Talk to the references yourself. Managers tend to be more honest and frank with other managers than they are with HR. Also, HR people are not the subject matter experts in your business area, therefore, you can ask the reference questions that HR can't.

❀ Consciously consider if the candidate's personality and temperament fit in well with your management style and the company's general atmosphere.

❀ My best hires over the years have always been smart people who are a quick study and have a great attitude. Don't necessarily pick the person with the best experience and/or credentials.

The things you shouldn't do.

❀ Don't go against your gut feel. Every time I've done that I've been sorry.

❀ If both people stink, don't hire one just because he or she is the better of the two possible evils. Start the process over and get more resumes to review.

❀ Don't make the decision solely on the candidate's salary requirements. If the right candidate is in the salary range, get the better person.

∼ Hiring Good People ∼

One of the hallmarks of a great manager is the ability to hire good people. Remember, as a manager, one major way you will be judged by your boss is how much you can be trusted to make good decisions. Decisions related to hiring are very visible and painful to correct.

∽ Key Points ∾

❈ For a manager, the hiring process is the combination of defining the job, getting permission to hire, working with a recruiter to find people, interviewing people, deciding which one you like, and presenting a job offer.

❈ There are many laws and regulations that must be followed during the hiring process. There are things you can and cannot say and/or ask.

❈ In office lingo, a job opening is very often called an "open requisition," abbreviated to "open req."

❈ A job description specifies the job's title, salary, job duties, eligibility requirements, and other similar information.

❈ Your job as the hiring manager is to be very supportive and helpful to the HR department. In other words, help them help you.

❈ Make sure to read the section in this book on how to review a resume (it's really good).

❈ One of the hallmarks of a great manager is the ability to hire good people. As a manager, you will be judged on your ability to make good decisions, especially hiring decisions.

❈ Decisions related to hiring are very visible and painful to correct.

CHAPTER 7

THE GOOD, THE BAD, AND THE OTHER

∽ Giving Promotions ∽

Giving someone a promotion sounds like it should be easy. You call the person into your office, tell her she has been promoted and to continue doing great work, shake her hand, and send her on her way. In one sense, it is that easy. However, there are a number of factors to consider when deciding whom to promote and when to promote them. Additionally, there are a number of ramifications associated with giving someone a promotion, and they're not all good. (Yeah, I know, you thought this one would be all good news. Well, welcome to management.)

Because you are a first-time manager, we'll concentrate on the types of promotions where you would be the decision maker, namely promotions in rank and title such as Programmer to Senior Programmer, Junior Buyer to Associate Buyer, and Junior Honcho to Head Honcho (just kidding).

When deciding if someone should be promoted, consider the person himself, his role within the department, the effect the promotion will have on the other members of the team, and the current department's situation.

Let's begin with the person himself. The first and most obvious question: is this person worthy of a promotion? The answer to this question involves the length of time he has been in the job, his competency, his attitude, his ability to perform the new level's required tasks, and your desire as his manager to promote him. Regarding his peers, you have to consider how other members of the team will react to this person's promotion. Will they agree and be supportive or will they be upset and/or feel the promotion was unwarranted and unfair? Regarding the department in general, if the department just failed on a major project, it's not a good time to promote someone no matter how good they are. Other thoughts such as "If I promote Joe, should I also promote Mary?" are very common and must be considered.

When you promote someone, you are telling that person and the rest of your team that the person being promoted embodies the desirable qualities, attitude, and attributes that facilitate recognition and promotion. As a result, you are telling the rest of your staff to act in the same manner.

> Promoting someone is the strongest statement you can make to the other people on your team as to how they should act if they would also like to be promoted.

Remember, promotions are not only a show of support and recognition toward the person who received it, they are also a statement and motivator (or de-motivator) to those who didn't get it.

Lastly, the decisions you make regarding who should and/or should not be promoted will be used by your boss to assess your decision-making ability. So, be fair, unbiased, and analytical when making promotion-related decisions. If not, you may find yourself being passed by on your next potential promotion.

∼ Parity in Pay among Peers ∼

The goal here is that everyone doing more or less the same job should receive more or less the same pay, with adjustments made based on experience and other appropriate factors.

That said, you would be shocked how differently people are paid, even within the same department, for doing basically the same work. I don't mean this in a divisive, prejudicial, or conspiratorial way. Very often, a person's professional and company history may affect their salary and the resulting pay discrepancy. For example, if Mike was hired when the job market was bad, and Mary was hired a year later when the job market was good, chances are that Mary will be making more money than Mike because Mary would not have joined the company at Mike's salary because she would have had other job offers.

As another example, Joe and Sally were both hired a year ago. Joe was hired as the manager of another department, and Sally was hired as a junior analyst. Joe then did a bad job managing his department and was moved into an individual contributor role as a Senior Analyst. Sally, on the other hand, did a great job and was promoted to Senior Analyst. Chances are the company did not reduce Joe's pay when he became an individual contributor. Chances are also good that Sally got an excellent raise, but is still below Joe's original manager salary.

The bottom line for you as the new manager is that Joe and Sally are basically doing the same job, but Joe is being paid a lot more than Sally. As the department manager, these are the kinds of pay problems you will have to address.

Your first goal as manager is to recognize that these issues exist. Your second goal is to work with your boss and HR to correct these issues. Generally, these issues tend to work themselves out on their own over time. As an example, let's look again at Sally and Joe. Over time, Sally will tend to get bigger raises than Joe because Sally is doing great work and is paid less than her peers. Joe on the other hand will tend to get less than average increases because he is being highly paid (maybe overpaid) for his current individual contributor job responsibilities.

If these types of pay differences become known by the members of your team, bad things can and probably will happen. If your best performers (like Sally in the last example) are making less money than your poor performers (Joe), then the individuals involved may start resenting each other, demand pay increases, and/or start looking for new jobs. Even worse, if anyone feels that these pay differences are due to discrimination, lawsuits may ensue. At best, lawsuits will cost your company money in legal fees alone, and they'll also generate bad press.

〜 Giving Raises 〜

As Tom Cruise said in the movie *Jerry McGuire*, "You complete me." Oh sorry, I meant, "Show me the money!" Yeah, that's the one, "Show me the money!"

Giving raises is not just about the money; it's also about the message behind the money. That said, my first suggestion is to never let someone find out about their pay raise by looking at his or her check stub or direct deposit balance.

The size of someone's pay raise can be meant as either a good thing or a bad thing. For example, is 3 percent a good raise? The short answer is maybe yes, maybe no. Let's put it in perspective using the following two sets of comments:

❊ "Hi, Mary. Congratulations on your 3 percent raise. I want you to know that the average raise this year was 2 percent. You got 3 percent because of your outstanding work over the past year."

Compare it to this statement:

❊ "Hi Mary. We gave you a 3 percent raise. I want you to know that the company did really well this year, and as a result, the average raise was 5 percent. You only received 3 percent because your work was not of the quality it has been in past years. Let's sit down next week and talk about an action plan that will help you return to your previous top performance."

Remember, job performance and salary discussions like these should always be done confidentially and in a nonpublic place such as an office or conference room. Also, particularly if you are giving someone bad news, make sure to leave time for them to ask questions, to tell their side of the story, and/or to vent their frustrations.

Before we continue, please note that this section doesn't discuss collective bargaining agreements, government employee salary rules, or other similar contractual agreements. It is written specifically to discuss how raises are given in privately and publicly held companies. In addition, this discussion also will not make you a salary planning expert; we'll leave that for HR. The goal here is to give you a general idea of how people's raises are decided. OK, now let's talk about who gets how much.

Pay raises are generally scheduled in one of two ways. Some companies give raises to people on the anniversary of their hire date. Other companies give everyone in the company a raise at the same time.

If your company gives people raises on their employment anniversary, then the math is simple. You will be given a general guideline/formula to follow that considers the person's performance, current salary, and other various factors. For the most part, you follow the formula and at the end, it tells you the raise amount. For example, let's consider a very simple formula in which top performers get a 5 percent raise, average performers get a 4 percent raise, below average performers get a 3 percent raise, and bad performers get no raise at all. Using this formula, if you consider the employee to be an average performer, he gets 3 percent. This simple formula is for illustration only and of course did not consider the person's current pay rate and other company specific factors.

If your company gives everyone pay raises at the same time, the math gets a little trickier. In companies of this type, you generally will also be given a guideline like the previous example. In this case, you will also be given a budget that represents the total pay increase for your department. This budget amount is generally calculated based on your department's total pay. For example, if you have five people in your department, and each one makes $20,000 a year, your department's total pay is $100,000. Now, if the HR department says that the average raise must be 4 percent, you will then have a $4,000 pay raise budget to divide among the members of your group.

The use of a budgeted raise amount has two major ramifications. First, if everyone in your department is making the same amount of money, if you give a 5 percent raise to one person, then you have to give someone else a 3 percent raise to stay within your $4,000 budget.

Second, presumably not everyone in your group is paid exactly the same amount. Therefore, the higher someone's salary is compared to the average, the greater effect it will have on your budgeted dollars. As an extreme example, say you have three people in your group: two make $20,000 each, and one makes $40,000. Therefore, like the last example, if the average raise is 4 percent, your total pay raise budget is $3,200. (That's 20,000 + $20,000 + $40,000 = $80,000; and 4% of $80,000 = $3,200).

In this first example, everyone is receiving a 4 percent raise, totaling $3,200 in total increases.

Name	Pay	Raise %	Raise $
Mary	$40,000	4%	$1,600
Joe	$20,000	4%	$800
Sally	$20,000	4%	$800
Total Raise Amount			**$3,200**

Now, if I give Mary (the person making $40,000) a 3 percent raise instead, I can give Joe and Sally (the people making $20,000) a 5 percent raise and still stay within my budget. This is shown below:

Name	Pay	Raise %	Raise $
Mary	$40,000	3%	$1,200
Joe	$20,000	5%	$1,000
Sally	$20,000	5%	$1,000
Total Raise Amount			**$3,200**

This also works the opposite way. If I want to give Mary a 5 percent raise, I have to give both Joe and Sally 3 percent raises.

Name	Pay	Raise %	Raise $
Mary	$40,000	5%	$2,000
Joe	$20,000	3%	$600
Sally	$20,000	3%	$600
Total Raise Amount			**$3,200**

Your job as the department manager will be to combine the math, team member performance, department goals, and company goals to create a pay raise plan that meets your budget and will be approved by your boss and HR.

∾ Span of Control Rules ∾

The term "Span of Control" can have many definitions, such as the level of responsibility a person has over a particular department or the decision-making authority in a specified business area or project. For our purposes, span of control refers to the number of direct reports a manager can personally manage effectively. The general rule of thumb is about seven people. In all honestly, I don't know if the number seven was decided upon by a scientific study, an author of a management book, or just generally agreed upon by gut feel. In any case, it feels about right.

Seven people may not sound like a lot to directly manage, but it is. When you consider that you have to oversee their work, mentor them, assure that each team member has enough to do, write annual (or semi-annual) performance reports, salary plans and bonus plans, deal with their professional and personal problems, and get your own work done, seven people is plenty.

If you have other personal job responsibilities, like helping customers directly, then managing more than four or five people can become unworkable.

I have seen departments where ten, fifteen, or even twenty people are reporting to one manager. Many members of these groups felt neglected, underappreciated, and in many cases, underutilized.

I'm not saying you should never manage more than seven people. What I am saying is that if your department has more than seven people, you should think about dividing it into teams, or at least have part of your group report to a team leader, who in turn reports to you. For example, if the accounting department has ten people, three working on General Ledger, three on Accounts Receivable, and four on Accounts Payable, you could have the best person in each area be a team leader, thus giving you three rather than ten direct reports. This approach not only gives you more time to do your work, but it also provides a career path for the people in your group.

Span of control and organization design could be a book by itself. My goal here is just to get you thinking about the topic and to have a general understanding of industry thoughts and practices.

∾ The Importance of Communication ∾

A common theme through many of the sections of this book has been the importance of communication with your group, your peers, your boss, your boss's boss, your customers, and just about anyone else that will listen. I wanted to discuss it here in its own section, to once again drive home the crucial role that good communication plays in your overall performance as a manager.

> Depending on your professional area and your personal strengths and weaknesses, good communication can be a difficult thing to achieve.

As an example, I went to school for accounting and computer information systems. Of the fifty classes I took as an undergraduate, only one optional elective dealt with personal communication (a public speaking class).

For many of us, we were told that we did such a good job as an individual contributor in our professional area of expertise, that we should take a new job as manager, a position for which we had no formal training and no on-the-job experience. Thus, a rookie manager was born.

By design, a manager's job is to manage people. This requires telling them what to work on and then providing them feedback on their job performance. It also requires that you provide upper management with the status of projects, accomplishments, and issues. At a department level, it's also your role to facilitate the coordination with other departments such as HR, finance, and your peer organizations. The bottom line is that the better you communicate, the easier it will be for you to become an effective manager.

One last thing (yeah, I know, there always has to be one last thing), by "communication," I don't mean talking about last night's New York Giants game against the Green Bay Packers, or perpetuating office gossip. I mean accurately and articulately conveying business-related material in an effective manner.

If continually communicating to other people is not a particular skill of yours, or if you just feel uncomfortable doing it, step outside your comfort zone and try it. You may find that over time, you grow to like it and as a result, get good at it. If you still have difficulty in face-to-face communication, where appropriate, use email.

∽ Contractor to Employee Conversions ∽

There are many occasions when it makes sense to bring in a temporary employee on a contractual basis. The reason may be that someone is on maternity leave, you may have a seasonal business, or you may be converting to a new computer system and simply need more hands for a month or two. Then, after assessing their actual job performance, you can decide to either let them leave at the end of their contract or hire them as a full-time employee.

Alternatively, there are many advantages of bringing in a potential employee as a contractor, and then based on their performance, deciding if you would like to hire them. In fact, this is a common practice in many companies. This is sometimes referred to as "temp-to-hire."

Sounds easy, right? You like someone's work, offer him a job, he says yes, he starts working for you as a regular employee, and all is well with the world. Right? Well, maybe. Many things can potentially make it difficult to convert a person from a contracting/temporary role to a permanent position.

Let's begin by discussing the contractual relationship between your company and the company that sent you the contactor. Of course, if you hired the person directly, without a contracting firm, this isn't an issue (wouldn't that be nice). When trying to hire people away from a contracting firm, the contracting firms generally fall into one of four categories: "No Way," "For a Price," "For a Shrinking Price," and "No Problem."

The "No Way" firms set up a contractual agreement with the companies they work with, stating that you cannot hire their contractors. They also have the people they represent (the contractor you would like to hire) sign a "non-compete" contract. This type of contract states that the employee cannot accept a job at the companies where they were placed as a contractor for a specified length of time, typically a year. If this is the case, you're stuck and cannot hire that person unless the contracting company owes you a favor (or you twist their arm really hard by threatening not to use any more of their contractors). I tend not to do business with these kinds of companies because I like the flexibility to hire someone who I think does good work.

The "For a Price" firms let you hire their contractors for a price. Generally, after a certain amount of time, typically three months to a year, you can hire their contractor for a specified finder's fee. The fee is typically based on a percentage of the contracting rate. This option gives you the flexibility to hire their people, but it can be very expensive.

The "For a Shrinking Price" firms let you hire their contractors at any time for a fee. The advantage here is that the fee gets smaller over time and is eventually eliminated, usually after six months or a year. The rational behind this arrangement is that it allows your company the flexibility to hire their people at any time, but allows their firm to be reasonably compensated for their efforts. This arrangement is fair to both companies, and I like doing business under this type of contract.

The "No Problem" firms let you hire their contractors as an accommodation to the companies they do business with. They ask you (either with a handshake or contractually) to keep the person as a contractor for a specified length of time, typically three or six months, before you hire them. This approach allows them to make a reasonable amount of revenue on the person before they are hired away. The basic difference between this arrangement and the "For a Shrinking Price" arrangement is the "For a Shrinking Price" firms have a pre-defined formula to hire people shortly after they start contracting. With a "No Problem" firm, short-time hires are generally worked out on a case-by-case basis. Very often, they will not charge you for a short-term hire if you promise to bring in an additional contractor to replace their revenue stream. Like the "For a Shrinking Price" type company, I also really like this approach because it gives you three to six months to decide if you like the person before you hire them, and then it gives you the flexibility to do so.

Sometimes it's not the company, but the individual, who slows or stops the contractor-to-employee conversion. Some people just like being contractors and do not want to be converted. Other people would like to stop contracting and become an employee, but can't afford the change in cash flow. Contractors are typically paid higher hourly rates than an employee, thus a bigger weekly paycheck. Of course, being an employee has other benefits like 401(k) matching, heath insurance and life insurance, and job stability, which can make employment more attractive than contracting, but the cash flow is usually less. If the contractor has high personal fixed costs, he may not be able to absorb the lower cash flow. If this is the case, with the help of HR, you may be able to work something out, or you may just not be able to hire him.

∽ Employee Training, Who Needs What ∽

Giving people training is both an employee right and a privilege. The employee thinks it's his right. His boss thinks it's a privilege.

It's been my experience that most companies agree that training is an important component of workforce productivity, employee morale, and company competitiveness. The questions arise over what type of training to provide, who gets it, and how much company time and money can be used to procure it.

From a budget perspective, training is generally categorized into two types, tuition reimbursement and seminar-based training. Tuition reimbursement is when the company pays for accredited college courses taken at night. In general, tuition reimbursement is considered (and budgeted) as an employee benefit, like life insurance, and its budget is not usually reduced midyear. Seminar-based training is generally not for college credit and is designed to teach a specific hard or soft skill.

Hard-skill-based classes teach a specific skill, like programming in Java or fixing a new type of refrigeration unit. Soft-skill-based training teaches things like time management, stress reduction, public speaking, and things of that nature. Going to user conferences generally falls under the "soft skill" umbrella even though that is not always accurate and/or fair.

A hard-skill-related class is usually easier to justify from a budget perspective if the class is needed to train an employee for an upcoming project because it gives the company a more tangible payback.

Generally, when companies go though their annual budget planning process, they usually include money for employee training. Training dollars are usually budgeted on a "per head" basis. In other words, during the budget process you will be told that each person in the company should be allocated a specified amount of training dollars, for example $3,000 a person. Therefore, if you have five people in your group, you will have a $15,000 training budget.

If the company does well that year, the training money stays in the budget. If the company does worse than expected, one of the first things to be cut is training dollars because it's a discretionary expense. This doesn't mean that companies feel that training is unimportant; it just means that it's an easy way to reduce short-term expenses. That said, if training is important to you and your group, send them to class early in the year while the dollars are still available.

In addition to paying big money for training classes, there are also many cost-effective ways (by cost-effective I mean cheap, oh no, did I say cheap, I meant inexpensive, yeah, inexpensive) to provide quality training. These include web-based training classes, free vendor-sponsored seminars, in-house classes sponsored by the HR department that have little or no cross charge, trade books, and CD/DVD-based training.

There are three big advantages of buying books and/or CD/DVD-based training. First, more than one person can use them. Second, they can be used as reference. Third, employees can read/listen to them at home on their own time, thus drastically reducing the loss of productivity associated with daytime-based training.

Now the questions of who receives training, who goes to the trade shows in fun far-away places, and so on. There is no generic answer for these, only a guideline, namely, be fair to your staff members but do what's right for the company. Additionally, be objective to the needs of the individuals in your group, assess the skill shortfalls within your department, and do what's right. That said, you should always find a way to provide at least some training for everyone, even if it's just an in-house class sponsored by HR, a day off from work to go to a free vendor-based local training class, or through the purchase of an appropriate how-to-type book.

One last thing to consider when defining your training budget—remember to budget the associated travel expenses. These expenses generally include car mileage if the person drives there for the day, or plane, hotel, rental car, and food expenses if the training (or user conference) is far away.

Lastly, remember to find the time and budget to take a training class yourself. Just because you're now a manager, it doesn't mean you should stop taking classes.

∾ Firing People ∾

Let's get the tough one out of the way up front. You can't just fire someone because you feel like it (even if you really, really want to). There are laws, federal regulations, state regulations, and company policies and procedures that must be followed. There is also the concept of protected classes based on age, sex, minority status, etc. My goal here is not to describe all of the rules and regulations you need to follow, but rather to tell you that lots of rules and regulations exist, and they differ from company to company, state to state, and country to country.

If you have any serious thought that a person should be terminated from the company, the first thing you need to do is discuss it with your boss. These are things you need to know before you go to HR. For example, is the guy your boss's best friend or his brother-in-law? You may also find that the person is simply the right guy in the wrong job and could find great success in another part of the company.

If your boss agrees that the person should be terminated, then you must go to HR. HR will help assure that you follow the correct procedures, fill out the right paperwork, and follow all the appropriate laws, regulations, and industry conventions. This correctness will help protect you and the company from lawsuits (or at least from losing lawsuits) and other unpleasant stuff. HR will also make sure you treat the person being fired with respect, fairness, and dignity. Remember, for you, firing this person is a business issue. For the person being fired, it is a life event and may cause hardships on him and his family.

∼ Laying People Off ∼

Unfortunately, layoffs are a reality in poorly performing companies. They are a way of reducing company expenses and thus increasing company profits. In today's business world, a company's stock often goes up when it announces layoffs because it shows Wall Street that the company is serious about reducing expenses.

> Some things about layoffs may seem counterintuitive. For example, the first time a company has a layoff, they tend to give the best severance packages.

The reason is that management feels guilty about laying people off. In addition, they probably have more money to expend during the first layoff, and then less to fund subsequent layoffs.

Should you be in the unfortunate situation of dealing with multiple rounds of layoffs, you will see that the company dynamics associated with the second and third rounds of layoffs is very different than the dynamics associated with the first round. The first round of layoffs, for the most part, removes the company's extra weight. As I say this, understand that I mean no disrespect to the people being let go. I have seen very talented people let go on the first round of layoffs. Most companies that have never had a reduction in force tend to have a number of people performing non-critical tasks. I stress that this is a timing issue, rather than a person issue. Their big project just ended or the product line they are selling is doing poorly. Things like that. That said, a layoff is also the opportunity to remove underperforming employees.

In general, the dynamic in the first round of layoff is described as "allowing the company to run lean-and-mean," "cutting out fat and redundancies," "streamlining operations," and so on. Most people are sorry to see their co-workers go, but understand that it was a necessary evil, and more importantly, that it wasn't them.

In the second and third rounds of layoffs, everyone within the company is nervous because all the low-hanging fruit is already gone. In anticipation of future rounds of layoffs, people will begin theorizing how the cuts will be done. Will they thin out middle management? Will they cancel specific projects and lay off the project members? Will they close a plant? Will they outsource particular business functions?

I have told you this general information about layoffs, because to effectively manage your department through a layoff, you have to have a general understanding of the environment.

As a department manager, you should have four primary responsibilities during a layoff. First, keep your department productive by keeping morale as high as possible. Second, decide who to lay off based on the company's best interest, rather than on personal feelings (this is very hard to do; in fact, it stinks—but it's what you're paid to do). Third, if you feel comfortable doing so, do everything in your power to help the people you laid off get new jobs (introduce them to your professional contacts, provide them with written references, etc.). Forth, and near and dear to your heart, try not to be laid off yourself.

One last piece of advice when dealing with your group during layoffs and other tough company times, ongoing communication is essential to your department's morale. I know I've said it before, but communicate often and communicate honestly. There is an old expression (I love old expressions, but I guess you know that by now) that the devil you know is better than the devil you don't. If people hear nothing, they will assume the worst. The last thing you need as a manager is to have your entire department looking for new jobs instead of doing their work.

∽ Key Points ∽

❋ When deciding if someone should be promoted, consider the person himself, his role within the department, the effect the promotion will have on the other members of the team, and the current department's situation.

❋ Parity in pay means that everyone doing more or less the same job should receive more or less the same pay, with adjustments made based on experience and other appropriate factors.

❋ Giving raises is not just about the money; it's also about the message behind the money.

❋ "Span of control" refers to the number of direct reports a manager can personally manage effectively. The general rule of thumb is about seven people.

❋ When trying to hire people away from a contracting firm, the contracting firms generally fall into one of four categories: "No Way," "For a Price," "For a Shrinking Price," and "No Problem."

❋ Giving people training is both an employee right and a privilege. The employee thinks it's his right. His boss thinks it's a privilege.

❋ From a budget perspective, training is generally categorized into two types, tuition reimbursement and seminar-based training.

❋ Hard-skill-based classes teach specific skills, like programming in Java or fixing a new type of refrigeration unit.

❋ Soft-skill-based training teaches things like time management, stress reduction, public speaking, and things of that type.

❋ There are three big advantages of buying books and/or CD/DVD-based training: more than one person can use them, the materials can be used as reference, and employees can read/listen to them at home on their own time.

❋ You can't just fire someone because you feel like it (even if you really, really want to).

❋ These are lots of rules and regulations associated with firing people. Work very closely with your boss and HR to make sure the rules are correctly followed.

❖ Be careful that the person you want to fire is not your boss's best friend or his brother-in-law.

❖ You may find that the person you wish to fire is simply the right guy in the wrong job and could find great success in another part of the company.

❖ Always remember, for the person being fired, it is a life event and may cause hardships on him and his family.

❖ As a department manager, you should have four primary responsibilities during a layoff; keep your department productive, decide who to layoff based on the company's best interest, do everything in your power to help the people you laid off get new jobs, and try not to be laid off yourself.

CHAPTER 8

HR AND VENDORS AND FINANCE (OH, MY!)

∾ Working with the Human Resources Department ∾

At any given time, the HR department can be your best friend, a royal pain in the neck, very helpful, and/or very frustrating. They can also flood you with paperwork, find people for you to interview, hire you, fire you, lay you off, or facilitate your promotion.

One of the most important things to know about HR is that they always work for your boss, no matter what level you are within the organization. Just as your HR representative is helping you with issues, paperwork, and staff planning, he is also helping your boss with the same set of activities. As an example, as you are working with HR to finalize pay raises for your subordinates, the same HR person is working with your boss to decide your pay raise.

On a day-to-day basis, it feels like the HR person works for you. He doesn't—he is a company resource provided to you, your peers, your boss, and other people in management. Remember, at one moment the HR person may be helping you screen resumes to fill a position in your department, and at the next minute, he may be sitting in a room with your boss helping him decide who to layoff.

The lesson here is that you want to have a good working relationship with your HR person. He will help you find people to hire, give you tips on writing performance reviews, assist you in salary planning, and maybe one day without you even knowing it, save your job.

As a general rule, I have found HR people to be great to work with. That said, to work with HR effectively, there are a few things that you have to remember. First, help them help you. In other words, certain managerial tasks require coordination with the HR group, such as hiring new employees.

> If your HR recruiter gives you ten resumes to look at, look at them in a timely manner and meet the defined HR deadlines for salary planning, bonuses, performance reports, and other similar activities.

HR didn't make up these deadlines for fun—senior company management approves the schedules for all company-wide initiatives, including the ones for HR. HR was told when the job had to be completed, and they need your help to do it. Also, bring HR in early on HR-related issues such as employee performance problems. Finally, understand that your HR representative is also working with other department managers. As a result, there will be times when you will have to compete for their attention.

∾ Working with Vendors ∾

I cannot overemphasize the importance of learning how to effectively work with vendors. You can save the company a lot of money by negotiating well, and by managing vendor-related projects well, you can help your department meet its deadlines.

When vendor-based projects go well, you can take credit; after all, you managed the vendor and the vendor relationship. If the project goes poorly, you did a great job; it was the vendor's fault.

Before discussing different types of vendors and specific vendor tactics, please note that there are entire books and professions built around purchasing, vendor relations, and other related fields. The goal here is to provide you with an introductory overview of the company-vendor relationship.

It is critical to understand the importance of dealing honestly and fairly with your vendors. Vendor relationships should be viewed as a win-win relationship. Namely, you are getting the goods and services you need at a fair price, with high quality and great customer service. The vendor, in return, should be getting reasonable contract terms and reasonable prices for their products. They should also be paid on time and dealt with in an honest and professional manner.

Strong relationships with your vendors are an asset to your company and an asset to you personally. Here are examples of each. Say your company has consistently paid its bills on time for years. If your company runs into a short-term cash flow problem and has trouble paying its bills, then your vendors will be more likely to *not* cut you off from product as quickly. As a second example, if a great-selling product is in short supply, then your vendors may give you the products first, giving you a leg up on your competition. On the personal side, if you lose your job (or just decide you want a new one), then your vendors can help you in two ways. First, you may have the opportunity to go to work for the vendor. Second, your vendors have contacts at lots of other firms in your industry and could help you meet people at these other companies.

I mentally categorize vendors into two types—providers, which are companies where you buy stuff (stuff of course being the technical term for business-related supplies and materials) and strategic partners who play an important role in your success or the success of the company. Examples of "provider" vendors are the office-cleaning company, your office-supply vendor (pens, paperclips, etc.), and the catering company that delivers company lunches. Examples of "strategic partner" vendors include companies that provide the raw materials for your products, offshore customer service centers, and software companies that support your core business processes.

> Provider-type vendors are generally judged on price, reliability, quality of customer service, and what I refer to as the pain-in-the-neck factor.

The only one of the items you can really negotiate is price. The vendor's internal workings and efficiency usually define the rest. Reliability is the vendor's ability to deliver the correct products on time. Quality of customer service is the ability to respond to your needs. For example, if they accidentally deliver the wrong printer toner, will they send you the right toner overnight express, at their expense, so your copy machines don't stop working? The pain-in-the-neck factor refers to how easy it is to deal with the vendor and how often they aggravate you. Examples of aggravating situations include taking four months to get your bill right, shipping the product to the billing address and sending the bill to the shipping address, having three different sales people call you on the same day, and making you fill out needless and/or redundant paperwork.

Here is the trick, when negotiating with provider-type vendors, beat them up on price based on problems you have had in reliability, quality of customer service, and pain-in-the-neck factors. Of course at some point, if the vendor just can't do the job, find a new vendor, even if it costs you a little more money.

Strategic-partner-type vendors are judged on different criteria, based on the product or service they provide. For example, if your company assembles pens, then it is very important for the ink cartridges to be delivered on time.

Generally speaking, negotiations with strategic-partner-type vendors include the creation of a Service Level Agreement (SLA). An SLA describes in detail the level of service that will be provided by the vendor. For example, a call-center-based SLA may specify that all incoming calls must be answered within three rings. Another SLA example is that specific raw materials must be delivered within a specified time after the order is placed. Very often the commitments specified in the SLA will have a major impact on the price. For example, a four-hour guaranteed response from a service vendor will generally cost more than a twenty-four guaranteed response. When dealing with strategic-partner-type vendors, cost is certainly always a factor. However, the vendor's ability to deliver is very often more important, because if the vendor fails, it will have an adverse effect on your customers and/or your internal company operations.

∽ Working with the Finance Department ∽

Companies are in the business of making money. Guess who counts it? You got it, it's the finance department. The key to working effectively with finance people is to understand their world. This is important because they measure your world, and you will be judged by their measurements. Your finance person can help you with a number of tasks, including building your initial annual budget, calculating your quarterly forecasts, and helping you analyze your actual revenues and expenses.

Additionally, if you ask real nice (say "please" and things like that), they can also generally give you very valuable advice on the best ways to manage your costs. I don't mean by telling you to stay in cheaper hotels (even though they do that too)—you can figure that one out on your own. What I mean is that a good understanding of how your company allocates revenues and expenses can greatly assist you in meeting your budget goals. For example, say you're buying lunch for ten customers who are coming to your office to discuss future software product changes. You may find that if you classify the lunch as a customer meeting, it's automatically charged to the marketing department rather than to your product development department. Of course the cost to the company is the same, but it saves your budget dollars for lunch on another day.

> As a manager, it's important for you to understand how your budget works, the effect that meeting (or missing) your budget has on your annual performance review, and should you receive one, the effect your budget results have on your annual bonus.

Your boss and your HR person can tell you the effect on your raise or bonus. The finance person, if asked, can help you assure (at least on the expense side) that your budgeted goals are met.

∼ Key Points ∼

❖ You want to have a good working relationship with your HR person. Your HR person will help you find people to hire, give you tips on writing performance reviews, assist you in salary planning, and maybe one day, without you even knowing it, he may save your job.

❖ To work with HR effectively, help them help you. Meet the HR deadlines for salary planning, bonuses, and other similar activities. Bring HR in early on HR-related issues.

❖ By negotiating well with vendors, you can save the company a lot of money, help meet company goals, and enhance your own career.

❖ Vendors can generally be categorized into two types— providers or strategic partners.

❖ A Service Level Agreement (SLA) describes in detail the level of service that will be provided by the vendor.

❖ The key to working effectively with finance people is to understand their world. This is true because they measure your world, and you will be judged by their measurements.

❖ Your finance person can give you very valuable advice on the best ways to manage your costs and the ins and outs of your budget.

CHAPTER 9

PROCESS TO THE PEOPLE (RIGHT ON!)

For those of you too young to get the "Right On!" joke, there was a song in the sixties that went "Power to the People, Power to the People, Right On!" For those of you who, like me, remember the song, sorry for having to spell it out. I know, it was a bad joke to begin with.

On a serious note, learning to properly handle employee-related paperwork and processes is important to you for two reasons. First, it's important to the people you manage. Think about it—isn't it nice when your boss takes the time to properly complete your paperwork? Same thing—except now you are the boss. Secondly, the proper handling of employee-related paperwork is now part of your job. As a result, you will be judged, in part, on your ability to perform these duties. This chapter discusses four key employee-oriented processes. Performance reviews are the primary written document for communicating and documenting the quality of an employee's work. Management by Objective is a goal-oriented management technique. Salary planning is the process that provides you, the manager, with the money needed to give your people pay raises. Lastly, succession planning is the process of naming your future replacement, hopefully because you are being promoted again!

∿ Performance Reviews ∿

Performance reviews are one of the most important things a manager can do for the people in his department. Take them seriously, complete them on time, and be honest, constructive, critical, complimentary, and sincere. Just like you have probably read and re-read your annual reviews, so will your subordinates.

Every company seems to have its own version of a performance review form. Some are all narrative-based, some are quantitative in nature, and most have components of the two.

Narrative-based performance reviews usually include a list of the person's prior year accomplishments, their strengths and weaknesses, a personal development/training plan for the coming year, and a short summary of the person's overall performance. Quantitative-based performance reviews are generally either a list of statements that you "strongly agree," "agree," "disagree," or "strongly disagree" with, or a list of attributes such as "leadership ability," "quality of work," and "timeliness" that you rate on a scale from one to ten.

> All review styles have the same intention, to provide the employees with an accurate and honest assessment of their personal performance during the prior year.

Additionally, the review should also be viewed as a basis for conversation between the manager and his subordinate.

If a person is doing a good job, they deserve to be told. If a person is doing a bad job, they also deserve to be told. In both cases, as their manager, it's your job to tell them. Furthermore, whether they are doing a good or bad job, it's also your job to tell them where improvements are needed. Then work with the person to formulate a plan to make those improvements. These plans generally include a combination of formal training classes, on-the-job experiences, and things to personally work on like attitude and level of effort.

I believe in the philosophy that "no one is so good that you can't find something that needs improvement, and that no one is so bad that you can't find something good to say in their review." When I write someone's review, regardless of the format, I make sure to discuss both their good points and their bad points. If you say only good things in a review, you may be helping their ego, but you are not providing them any tangible value; as a result, you are really doing the person a disservice. If you only say bad things, even if they are meant in a constructive way, the person will just feel beat up and not take your criticism to heart.

A good review is hard to write. As a result, not all managers take the time and effort required to do them properly.

It's easy to whip up something that says someone is great. It's difficult to write constructively about what people are doing wrong. As a result, many managers don't bother. Don't be one of those managers. The people on your team worked for you all year, they certainly deserve an hour or two of your time to write an appropriate annual review.

Now let's turn on radio station WIFM (What's In it For Me?). Writing a good review for your people is actually very good for you and your career. First, the people in your group will appreciate your effort and as a result will most likely be a little more loyal to you. Second, you want to be known as a good manager, and good managers write good reviews. Third, it's always a good idea to impress the HR guy. HR people know which managers write good reviews and which managers couldn't be bothered. Fourth, if the constructive criticism in your employees' reviews improves their performance, then your department will run more efficiently. Fifth, if someone in your group is performing poorly, their annual review serves as documentation that will assist you in removing them. Sixth, if you gain a reputation of being a good manager, it will be easier for you to hire quality internal candidates.

The annual (or semi-annual) performance cycle is generally done in one of two ways. Reviews are either done on the anniversary of each person's date of hire or all at once. If they are done all at once, block out a lot of time on your calendar or you will never get it done.

Generally speaking, pay raises are given in association with, or shortly after, the performance review process. This is advantageous to both you and the company. From the company's perspective, they want to give raises to their best performers. What better way to know who is performing well than to have everyone's annual performance review in hand. It is good for the manager because she can justify why she wants to give people good or bad raises without having to write a whole new performance review. For pay-raise specifics, refer to Chapter 7.

∿ Management by Objective (MBOs) ∿

Not all companies do MBOs, but I wanted to discuss them because you may eventually see them. Whereas a performance review looks at the year that just ended, MBOs look at the year ahead. Another name for MBOs could be "stuff I promise to do next year" or "things I have to do if I want my bonus," but MBO sounds much more professional.

Generally speaking, at the manager level, MBOs usually contain a combination of departmental goals and personal goals. Examples of departmental goals include "reduce bill processing time to five days" or "implement a new accounting system." Examples of personal goals include "take a time management class (if you have the time)" or "visit the Boston and San Diego offices." Then, at the end of the year (or at bonus time, based on your company's schedule), your boss will review your MBOs, and a decision will be made as to whether or not you met your objectives.

Here is the thing with MBOs, if the business environment changes during the year, your MBOs will not be met, and it's not your fault. For example, say you have an MBO to visit the Boston office and the office closes, you obviously can't go there. Thus, you should not be penalized for not going to Boston. (By the way, if you go to Boston, have dinner in the North End, the Italian food is incredibly good.)

Departments are generally either process-oriented or project-oriented. Process-oriented departments do have some discreet projects, but they primarily perform the same set of tasks all year. For example, the payroll department spends its whole year processing payroll. Project-oriented departments, like software development groups, do have some process-based tasks, but primarily spend their time on software projects. That said, MBOs in process-oriented departments tend to hold their relevance through the year, because for the most part, their MBOs will be process-improvement based.

MBOs in project-oriented departments tend to lose their relevance because very often business decisions are made that dramatically change the list of projects. For example, if a software development department manager has an MBO to build an HR system, and the new VP of HR decides he likes the old system, then the new system will not be built. Thus, the MBO to build the new HR system is now irrelevant.

I have one last item about MBOs that I would like to pass your way. Make sure that your MBOs are consistent with your boss's MBOs and your subordinate's MBOs. If they are, your MBOs will be a lot easier to make.

∼ Salary Planning ∼

In this section, rather than discuss individual pay raises, which I did in Chapter 7 (see "Giving Raises"), I will be talking about the salary-planning process in general.

My goal here is not to make you a salary-planning expert. As with the other sections, we'll leave that to the HR and compensation professionals. The goal here is for you to gain a general understanding of various salary-planning fundamentals. These fundamentals include "job descriptions," "job levels," "salary ranges," "salary surveys," and "position in salary range."

A "job description" is a description of the job, including its title (the name of the job, example, Business Analyst), responsibilities, tasks, needed skills, required certifications, and needed level of experience. As discussed in the "Hiring Process" section of this book, the job description is the primary communication vehicle that goes out to your boss, HR, and potential candidates regarding the job's responsibilities.

> The job description is also the basis for defining the job's "level" and "salary range."

A "job level" is where the job fits within the company's job hierarchy. For example, the Business Analyst job family may go from "Junior Business Analyst" to "Senior Business Analyst" to "Principal Business Analyst." As a result, the job description for a Senior Business Analyst should require more experience than the job description for a Junior Business Analyst.

Once a job is leveled within the company, it has to be assigned a "salary range." A salary range is the range of pay that the company is willing to pay for the job. For example, the range of pay for a Junior Business Analyst may be from $40,000 to $60,000, and the range of pay for a Senior Business Analyst may be from $50,000 to $70,000. Conceptually, these salary ranges are determined by a number of factors, including needed skills, required certifications, amount of experience, and level of responsibility.

In reality, the salary range associated with a job tends to be driven by general market conditions, supply and demand for the specified skill set, and what other local companies are paying for similar jobs. As an added point, sometimes specialized skills demand higher salary ranges. For example, knowledge in new computer software technologies tends to bring a higher price than the equivalent skills in standard or older technologies.

Many HR departments define their salary ranges with the help of "salary surveys." These surveys are facilitated by consulting firms that collect, aggregate, and analyze salary data from hundreds of companies. Then, they summarize the collected information by job type and sell it back to the participating companies. The companies then use it as a reference guide to define their salary ranges.

Once a job's salary range has been defined, the general rule of thumb regarding where a person should be "positioned in a salary range" is that a person new to the job (by new, I mean less experienced) should be paid in the lower end of the salary range. Then, as the person gains experience and becomes fully qualified, his pay should be in the middle of the range. Lastly, as the person becomes very experienced in the position, his pay should be in the higher end of the range.

Some companies break salary ranges into quartiles. Quartiles are four smaller ranges within the salary range. For example, as discussed earlier, if the Junior Business Analyst salary range goes from $40,000 to $60,000, the quartiles would be $40,000 to $45,000, $45,001 to $50,000, $50,001 to $55,000, and $55,001 to $60,000.

With the range quartiles defined, a person's pay raise is then partially based on their quartile within the range. The rationale being, that if you are fully qualified for the job, you should be at midpoint of the salary range, in this case, $50,000. Thus, if you are fully qualified (and doing a good job) and paid less the $50,000, you are underpaid and should receive a larger than average increase. Conversely, if you are making more than $50,000, you should get a smaller increase because you are already being appropriately compensated. The chart below is an example of a salary-planning guideline that combines job performance and salary quartile (position in the salary range).

Job Title:	Junior Business Analyst
Salary Range	$40,000 – $60,000
Average Pay Increase Percent:	5%

	Poor	Below Avg.	Average	Above Avg.
Quartile 1: $40,000 to $45,000	0%	3%	6%	7%
Quartile 2: $45,001 to $50,000	0%	2%	5%	6%
Quartile 3: $50,001 to $55,000	0%	1%	4%	5%
Quartile 4: $55,001 to $60,000	0%	0%	3%	4%

Then, reviewing the above salary raise matrix, you will see two blended themes. First, the better your performance, the higher your raise. Second, the lower your quartile, the higher your raise.

Sorry for all the math and numbers, but welcome to management. For some new managers, like accountants and computer programmers, these numbers are easy. For people who are less math-oriented, you have to learn to do this stuff—it is part of your job. However, I have a suggestion for the mathematically challenged; don't be afraid or intimidated by the numbers. Whether it is salary planning, budgeting, or another managerial task, it has to be done. Therefore, ask for help from your HR and/or finance person. It's their job to help you.

∼ Succession Planning ∼

Lucky you, you get to plan for your own replacement. This is both a good thing and a bad thing. Let's begin by talking about the good stuff. First, your boss will also be planning for his replacement, which may one day mean a promotion for you. Second, if you can't be replaced, then you can't be promoted. Logic dictates that the company can't give you a different/better job if they can't find anyone else to do your old job. The down side is that succession planning helps the company remove you if they are so inclined. The truth is that if they want to fire you or lay you off, they are going to do it with or without a formal succession plan. The only truly bad thing about succession planning is it doesn't feel good to discuss it with your boss. My answer to you, get over it.

Now let's talk about succession planning as a corporate activity, rather than how it affects you personally. If done correctly, succession planning is a company-wide activity that documents a replacement for every manager and key individual contributor in the company. This plan gives management the information needed to effectively restructure, grow, and/or shrink the company. It also provides insight into how to promote, reassign, fire, and/or replace key company employees.

For example, a company may need five managers to staff a new project. The succession plan will help senior management decide how to backfill the people being moved. As a second example, a manager (maybe even you) has accepted a position at another company, and your boss needs to replace him. The succession plan provides a starting point in the replacement process.

∾ **Key Points** ∾

❀ Performance reviews are one of the most important things a manager can do for the people in his department. Take them seriously, complete them on time, and be honest, constructive, critical, complimentary, and sincere.

❀ Narrative-based performance reviews include prior year accomplishments, strengths and weaknesses, personal development/training plans, and overall performance.

❀ Qualitative-based performance reviews are either a list of statements that you "strongly agree," "agree," "disagree," or "strongly disagree" with, or a list of attribute such as "leadership ability," "quality of work," and "timeliness" that you rate on a scale from one to ten.

❀ When you write someone's review, make sure to discuss both their good points and their bad points.

❀ At the manager level, Management by Objective or MBOs usually are a combination of departmental goals and personal goals.

❀ Make sure that your MBOs are consistent with your boss's MBOs and your subordinate's MBOs. If they are, your MBOs will be a lot easier to make.

❀ Salary-planning fundamentals include "job descriptions," "job levels," "salary ranges," "salary surveys, and "position in salary range."

❀ Many HR departments define their salary ranges with the help of "salary surveys" facilitated by consulting firms that collect, aggregate, and analyze salary data from hundreds of companies.

❀ If you can't be replaced, then you can't be promoted.

❀ If done correctly, succession planning is a company wide activity that documents a replacement for every manager and key individual contributor in the company.

CHAPTER 10

BUDGETING

This section takes a very narrow view of budgeting. It specifically concentrates on the issues, responsibilities, and activities that you will have as a "cost center manager." That is, as a manager responsible for his department's expenses. Additionally, this discussion deals only with the expense side of your budget and does not discuss budgeted revenue, also known as sales forecasts.

When reading this section, you will see that I use the word "budget" in two ways. I have done this on purpose, because it is used in two ways in business. The first way, which is the most obvious, is as your "budget," or the amount of money you plan to spend during the year, broken out by expense type. The second use of the word "budget" is as a comparison of your budgeted expenses versus your actual expenses. As an example, the question "How are you doing on your budget?" can mean two different things depending on the time of year. If your boss asks you this question during the budget-planning process, he is most likely asking if you have finished planning/drafting next year's budget. If your boss asks you the same question in the middle of the year, he is most likely asking you if your actual expenses are above or below your budgeted expenses (budgeted vs. actual).

∿ Importance of Your Budget ∿

Your department's budget is enormously important on a number of different levels. The first and most obvious is company profitability. Certainly your department's budget alone will not make or break the company's success, but the combined budget of all departments certainly will. Second, making your budget objectives is very important not only to your boss, but also your peers. It's important to your boss because your budget is part of his budget. If your department spends more money than it should, then your boss has to make up the difference somewhere else. Basically, your boss has to take budget dollars away from one of your peers.

Now let's talk about you. Your department's budget is important to you for two reasons. First, your budget is the vehicle that allows you and your group to take training classes, have department lunches, attend user conferences, buy needed equipment, and go to faraway cities to have face-to-face meetings with your clients and vendors. In other words, if you use your budget effectively, you can enhance your department's productivity and effectiveness. Your budget is also important to you personally, because if you meet your budget goals, you will most likely get a bigger bonus.

∿ Components of Your Budget ∿

When reviewing your department's budget, you will find that the items within it can be categorized into one of three types based on your control over them. These categories are "No Control," "Some Control," and "Full Control." Before I explain these three categories, please note that they are not accounting or finance terms. In fact, the accounting and finance managers reading this book may not be able to decide if my categorizations are brilliant and insightful or funny, but they are very true.

"No Control" items are costs that you have virtually no control over. These expenses are typically allocations of overhead costs such as occupancy (rent, heat, electricity, etc.). These costs are generally allocated based on either the actual or forecasted number of employees in your group. Since you have no control over what the company pays for rent, you can't really be judged on these costs. However, if these costs go up dramatically, you may be required to adjust other items in your budget to stay within your overall budget. It's the finance department that calculates the allocations. Therefore, your finance person may be able to find a way to minimize the effect of these items on your total budget or at least make sure that you are not penalized for it at bonus time.

> Your finance person is your best line of defense against problems with "No Control" items.

"Some Control" items are costs that you have a limited ability to control. Examples of these expenses include payroll, telephone bills, and vendor agreements. Regarding your payroll expense, you obviously have to pay your people, but you can delay hiring. Delaying a hire by a month or two has a very positive effect on your expenses. It not only reduces your actual expense by the salary amount, but it also reduces the costs of benefits, payroll taxes, and headcount-based allocations.

Regarding your department's telephone expense, generally speaking, you can't save too much here, but there is one thing to consider. Keep an eye on your international calling costs. If your company doesn't make international calls as part of its business, then they may not have an international calling plan. That said, all you need is one person in your department with a family member or significant other in a faraway country to totally destroy your budget.

The amount of control you have over vendor costs largely depends on the type of service, the type of vendor, and the type of contract. Vendors are discussed in Chapter 8, so I won't go into detail here. But from a budget perspective, vendor costs can easily make or break your budget. Strong negotiations with a vendor can have a very positive effect on your budget and truly save the company a lot of money. If you are not an experienced negotiator, enlist the assistance of someone who can help or mentor you. I would suggest asking your boss, someone in the company's purchasing group, a corporate lawyer, or a peer whom you trust. Don't let them do the negotiation for you; if you do it with their help, then you will gain very valuable experience.

Generally speaking, the "Some Control" items will be the biggest piece of your budget. Therefore, small percentage savings in this area can give you a lot of flexibility in other areas of your budget.

"Full Control" items include items such as training, travel (airplanes, hotels, food, etc.), user conferences, professional dues, lunches for in-house meetings, and expenses for offsite meetings. Unless your department does a lot of required travel, the "Full Control" items tend to be a small percentage of the overall budget, but they're the easiest to cut when times get tight. Think of it from a personal perspective. It makes more sense to reduce your personal expenses by bringing lunch rather than by not paying your rent.

∽ Budget Planning Process ∽

The budget planning process is generally done on an annual basis, with analysis versus actual done monthly and budget forecasts and adjustment done quarterly.

For the example I am about to present, let's assume that the company's fiscal year (their financial year) goes from January 1st to December 31st. This being the case, the annual budget cycle probably begins in September for really big companies and in October or November for medium-size companies. The larger the company, the more complex the budget, and the earlier they have to start. The reason that budgets in large companies are more complex is because there are more people, organizations, locations, and currencies involved.

Let's say the budget process starts in October. The first step in the budget process is the finance people rolling their eyes and saying, "Wow, I can't believe it's budget time already. Between planning next year's annual budgets and calculating this year's actual year-end numbers, I'll be here ten hours a day until the end of January."

The first step that you, as a manager, will see in the annual budget planning process is an email (or memo) describing the steps you must follow to complete your budget. This email will include general budget guidelines, step-by-step instructions on each budget phase, a description of the software used to collect the budget information (which very likely will be Excel), and the dates by which each step must be completed. Pay very close attention to this email and do exactly what it says. Remember, your next bonus and/or pay increase will at least be partially based on your ability to meet your budget numbers.

If you mess up the budget, not only will you upset your boss and the finance department, you will also be paying for it all year long.

Generally speaking, the budget process will have two (or more phases). The first phase, ending the beginning of November, will be you documenting how many people and how much money you need in the upcoming year. The second phase, due about the end of November, will be you cutting new hires and money out of your budget because your boss and/or the finance group told you to make your budget smaller.

I'll discuss this more in the "Padding Your Budget" section, but the moral of this story is to ask for more than you think you will need in the first budget round, so when you are asked to reduce your budget, you still have a reasonable level of funding.

Hopefully, the company's annual budget will be finalized by the end of December. Very often, however, the budget process takes longer than expected, and you may not get your final budget numbers until January.

With the annual budget process complete and the new year upon you, you will get your January month-end actual numbers the beginning of February. This will be your first indication of how well you've budgeted. Review all the numbers with your finance person to make sure that you understand their source, effect on your budget, and expected run-rate through year-end, and that you are not being over-charged/ cross-charged in error. It is very important to do this in January because budgets never seem to be created perfectly and very often adjustments are made as late as the end of February. If you find the problems early, you may be able to correct them and not have to live with them all year.

> The process of reviewing your budget compared to actual numbers should be done as soon as possible each month.

You don't want to wait until the end of the year to review your budget numbers. Telling your boss in November that you have been over budget all year and didn't know it would be very unpleasant for both of you.

In addition to the monthly cycle discussed above, there is also a quarterly cycle, particularly if you work for a publicly held company. This is because publicly held companies report their earnings to Wall Street on a quarterly basis. The additional work performed quarterly would be to forecast and/or modify your budget based on business conditions and/or changes in company priorities. For example, if the company is not doing as well as expected, you may be asked to reduce your budget.

Then, come next October, you too will be saying, "Wow, I can't believe it's budget planning time already. Where did the year go?" Hopefully you will also say, "Wow, I'm about 10 percent under budget this year. I bet I'll get a great annual bonus. I'm glad I listened to all that great advice in Eric's book. I think I'll tell all my friends to buy it." (I know, a shameless plug for my book. What can I say? Sorry—well, not really.)

∽ Padding Your Budget (I Mean Creating Budget Contingency) ∽

Forecasting the year ahead is a very hard thing to do. Business conditions change. Low-cost suppliers go bankrupt. New hires require higher salaries than originally anticipated. The cost of gasoline and jet fuel go up, therefore travel is more expensive than originally planned. As a result, many managers try to pad their budgets with a certain amount of unplanned but plausible expenses, so they can meet these unexpected business challenges without totally messing up their budgets.

This is not done to fool the company in any way—it's done because experience has shown that you can't plan for every contingency, and therefore you need a little room in your budget to meet unexpected challenges. For example, if you have ten projects planned for the coming year, experience tells you that for technical, vendor, business, or market-based reasons, one to two of these projects will require more resources than originally planned. Providing for this contingency is good for the company and will help your boss get you the resources needed to meet these unseen challenges.

Here are some commonly used techniques that I have heard of in the past. (By the way, if you are my finance person, friends with my finance person, or closely related to my finance person, please don't read this and skip to the next section. Just kidding.)

Budget padding opportunities:

- ❀ If you think you will need to hire people in June, budget them for March. Should you need them earlier than expected, you have the budget dollars. If you hire them when originally anticipated, you have three months worth of salary and benefits added to your contingency budget.
- ❀ If you think you will need to hire five people, budget for seven people. Should you need them, you have the budget dollars. If you hire the planned number of people, you have the salary and benefits for two others to use later.
- ❀ If you plan to travel once every two months, budget a trip every month instead. This will give you the flexibility to travel

more often if business requires it. It also allows you to bring someone with you if additional support is needed. Also, if travel costs are greater than expected, you can still make the required number of trips.

❖ Budget ample money per person for training. This allows for the ideal—that everyone can have proper training—but this rarely ever happens, thus allowing additional training dollars for select individuals.

❖ If you have international operations, assume a worsening exchange rate. If you're right, then you have the money in the budget to absorb it. If you're wrong, then you have extra budget dollars.

❖ Assume you will need to purchase more supplies/materials than you think you will need. If you are right, then you have the money in the budget to do it. If you're wrong, then you have extra budget dollars.

At first glance, this may sound deceitful, but the truth is that inexperienced managers tend to be overly optimistic. As a result, they underestimate needed budget dollars. Underestimating a project is a huge disservice to your company, your boss, and yourself. From a company perspective, decisions to do projects are made based on their return on investment. If you underestimate the cost, then by definition you are overestimating the return on investment. From your boss's perspective, to complete your projects, he may have to move needed dollars away from other worthwhile projects. From your perspective, if you continually come in over budget, then you will hurt yourself professionally.

∼ Expenses Versus Capitalization ∼

I'll start this section by saying, I'm not a lawyer or a CPA, but I did play one on TV (I really didn't, but I always wanted to say that). That said, I would like to explain the difference between expenses that have to be expensed and expenses that can be capitalized. Your first thought may be "Who cares?" The answer is your company's senior management and finance group may really care.

At a high level, a company can spend money in one of two ways, as either a current period expense, or as a long-term investment. Money spent as a current period expense must be deducted in the current period. Money spent as a long-term investment (or capital expenditure) is capitalized, meaning that rather than being expensed in the current period, it is placed on the balance sheet as an asset and then depreciated.

You may now ask, "Why do I care?" The answer is twofold. First, if the expense is categorized as a capital expenditure, there is the potential for tax credits. Second, if the company is publicly held, capitalization of expenses not only increases current net income, but it also increases the company balance sheet.

If you have the background to understand what I'm talking about, that's great. If you don't, then don't worry about it. In either case, I strongly suggest that you ask your finance person if any of your department's expenses can be capitalized. If the finance person says the expenses can be capitalized, and the company wants them to be, carefully follow the capitalization instructions specified by the finance person. These instructions must be followed carefully because the company may one day be audited to assure that proper capitalization rules were followed.

Now, you are probably wondering why I discussed capitalization in a section about budgeting. Here is the trick. If an expense is capitalized, it may not affect your budget the same way. Thus, reducing your department's expenses and with luck, increasing your annual bonus.

∼ Key Points ∼

❀ The items in your department's budget can be categorized into one of three types: "No Control," "Some Control," and "Full Control."

❀ "No Control" items, like occupancy, are costs that you have virtually no control over.

❀ "Some Control" items, like telephone expenses, are costs that you have a limited ability to control.

❀ "Full Control" items, like travel, are costs that you have full ability to control.

❀ Many managers try to pad their budgets with a certain amount of unplanned but plausible expenses so they can meet unexpected business challenges without totally messing up their budgets.

❀ Take a second look at the various ways to pad your budget.

❀ A company can spend money in one of two ways, either for use in the current period or as a long-term investment. Money spent as a current-period expense must be deducted in the current period. Money spent as a long-term investment (or capital expenditure) is capitalized.

CHAPTER 11

MANAGEMENT NO-NO'S

∼ No, Don't Do It ∼

This section is a little shorter than the other sections because all of the topics have the same advice. The advice is "No, don't do it." Should you decide not to follow that advice, proceed at your own peril.

Just for fun, there is one topic in this section that's OK to consider, but not to act on.

As you read this chapter, you'll see that I'm big on being honest and doing the right thing. You should be, too. (Sorry if I sound like your mother, but I bet she would agree with me that "honesty is the best policy." Oh, wow, now I sound like *my* mother.)

∽ Playing Favorites ∽

By favorites, I mean giving a specific employee preferential treatment. It's human nature to like some employees more than others. Many life-long friendships began as manager and subordinate. Personal friend-ship between a manager and a subordinate only becomes a problem when the manager openly and clearly has one set of rules for his friend and another set of rules for everyone else. As the manager, you must treat all your subordinates fairly and equally. If you don't, the other members of your team will resent it. This resentment has the potential to hurt productivity, create infighting within your staff, cause your group to lose respect and confidence in you, and ultimately cause peo-ple to leave. Lastly, it will be harder for you to hire internal candidates because they know they will be treated as a second-class citizen within the department.

In the long run, playing favorites can drastically reduce your effec-tiveness. When you're in the office, business is business, and all staff should be treated equally. Remember, ultimately it's your career that will suffer.

∾ Gossiping about Your Staff ∾

My suggestion is to not gossip at all. I know it's fun. It's also interesting to hear the gossip that's going around the office. The good news about gossip is it can also help keep you in tune with what's going on around the company.

The first lesson here is that it's fine to listen to gossip; it's not such a good idea to perpetuate it.

There is an important distinction between gossiping about your peers and/or managers and gossiping about your staff. When you gossip about your staff, it is taken as fact, not as gossip. The reason is that it's your job to know what your staff is doing. So if you say it, it must be true.

A second reason not to gossip about your staff is because you're their manager. Your job is to protect your subordinates and treat them with respect. Would you want your manager to gossip about you? Also, there are times when employees confide in their managers about health, family, and personal problems that may affect their work. Discussing these personal issues with other people is a breach of trust. Should you do so, you will hurt both your subordinate and yourself. Having his information disclosed hurts your subordinate. You have hurt yourself by showing the company that you are not trustworthy.

∽ Lying to Your Staff ∽

If you don't want your staff to lie to you, then don't lie to them. As manager of the group, you set the department's mood, rules, and common practices. The people in your group talk to each other. Therefore, if you lie to one of them, he or she will eventually figure it out and make sure your whole staff knows. The ultimate result will be your staff's loss of trust in you.

∾ Lying to Your Boss about Your Staff ∾

How does this sound? If you lie to your boss, you very possibly will lose your job. If the lie is big enough, you will lose your job as soon as your boss figures it out. If the lie is not big enough to get you fired immediately, then your boss will eventually get rid of you anyway. Personally, I don't like managing people I can't trust. I always treat my staff with honesty and respect and expect the same in return.

Regarding lying to your boss about your staff, why would you? If you are protecting a staff member from getting in trouble, you have just implicated yourself in their misdoing. If you lie to your boss by taking credit for something that a staff member did well, then you are stealing that person's credit. In both cases, you are showing yourself to be untrustworthy, and you will eventually lose the support of your boss and the loyalty of your team. Lastly, if your boss asks you a question about a specific person in your group, he may already know the answer. So be honest.

∾ Lying to Human Resources about Anything at All ∾

If you want to get sued or fired, then lie to HR. The only reason you would ever have to lie to HR is if you did something wrong and don't want to tell them. So let's see, what did you do? Did you make a promise to an employee that you should not have made? Did you make an oral job offer to a job applicant before you got the OK from your boss and/or HR? Did you mess up someone's pay raise? Do you get the idea?

HR is there to help us with HR issues, even if we accidentally caused them. Lying to HR is like lying to your boss—it will eventually come back to haunt you.

> If you accidentally caused an HR-related issue (or nightmare), you will need HR's help to fix it. So fess up and tell them what you did.

∾ Leaving Employee Data Hanging Around ∾

This topic is just a heads-up about not accidentally doing something dumb. As an individual contributor, if you handled sensitive data, it was most likely data about your clients. As a manager, you will be handling data about people inside your own company. Here is the lesson—make sure you handle internal company data very carefully.

As discussed in the section on employee pay raises, it is very common for people performing basically the same job to be paid very differently. As a result, if your team walks into your office for a staff meeting and all of their salaries are sitting face-up on your desk or displayed on your screen, major employee issues could quickly arise.

When you leave your office, even to go get coffee, get in the habit of turning on your computer screen saver and checking what's on your desk. You don't have to be paranoid about it, just smart. As a manager, you will be handling various types of sensitive company and employee documents. These documents include salary-planning documents, performance reviews, tuition reimbursement forms, and new hire offer letters. It is best to keep them as private as possible.

A number of years ago, I worked in an office designed in a way that when sitting at my desk, my back was toward the door. Even worse, my computer screen was also facing the door. I was working on a subordinate's annual performance review, and another subordinate quietly walked into my office and started reading it over my shoulder. When I finely saw him, he said he wasn't looking at my computer screen. He said he just didn't want to interrupt me. It was very obvious he was not being completely honest. From that time forward, I have tried to point my computer screen way away from my office doorway.

∼ Making Promises to Your Staff that You Can't Keep ∼

When you promise something to an employee, they take it as a done deal. For example, if you promise a promotion to a staff member at the completion of a project, he will be expecting his promotion at project end. If you can't deliver, then at best, you have lost credibility; at worst, the employee will be on his way to HR to complain.

As another example, if you tell a staff member that if he works through the weekend, he can go to an upcoming user conference, and then you don't let him go, not only will you lose personal credibility, but you will also never get the person to work another weekend.

By making promises you can't keep, I don't mean to imply that you are purposely lying to your staff. I mean that you should carefully consider your ability to keep to your side of the bargain. That said, if you continually fail to follow through on your promises, even if a promise is made with the best intentions, you will eventually be viewed as either a liar or ineffective.

∼ Sexual Harassment ∼

As a manager, you are in a position of power over your subordinates. Be very careful and respectful as to what you say, what you do, and what you imply. If you're a "touchy" person or a flirt by nature, keep it out of the office. Even if your advance is not intentional and is not meant in an offensive way, it may be interpreted differently.

One person's slap on the butt can be another person's lawsuit.

A sexual harassment complaint against you will, at a minimum, be very embarrassing and seem to follow you through your career. At worst, you will be fired, sued, and disgraced, not to mention what your significant other will have to say about it.

It's true that a sexual harassment suit against you would be very unpleasant, but remember, sexual harassment is against the law for a reason. The reason is because of the unfair position and distress it places on a subordinate, peer, or other company members.

If you have any question about sexual harassment, ask your HR person for a quick lesson. Most of it is common sense and obvious, but some of the rules are rather subtle. For example, as a manager, you don't have to harass a person directly, you only have to foster an environment where sexual harassment is encouraged and/or tolerated.

∼ Making Racial, Sexual, or Other Jokes in Bad Taste ∼

Hey, did you hear the joke about the you-know-who that did the you-know-what? Did you hear the joke about the guy who told a racial joke in the office and lost his job? How about the joke about the guy who told a sexually oriented joke in the office and was sued for sexual harassment?

Off-color jokes have an interesting way of unexpectedly offending people. Sometimes it's because a co-worker is a member of the group being picked on. Sometimes it's because you're making needless fun of a group or type of person that a co-worker loves. Then again, there are simply a lot of people who hate jokes that hurt people.

My advice to you is to keep dirty jokes, racial jokes, and all other inappropriate jokes and comments out of the office.

You should also avoid sending dirty jokes via email. Not only can it be easily forwarded without your knowledge, it also permanently documents the fact that you sent the joke through the office. For the record, emails can be used as an exhibit in a lawsuit. (How about that? I didn't even say that "I'm not a lawyer, but I did play one on TV." Sorry, I couldn't stop myself from using that bad joke just one more time, but at least it's not dirty.)

∽ Having Sex with a Subordinate ∽

No matter how much you want to date a subordinate, don't do it. Unless you live happily ever after, then life in the office may become very uncomfortable. Think of it this way, how would you like to spend eight hours a day for the next year with your ex-boyfriend or ex-girlfriend? I didn't think so.

There are other reasons why you don't want to sleep with a subordinate. First, it may be against company policy, and you could lose your job. Second, you are opening yourself up to a future sexual harassment complaint. Third, if you're married, then it's obvious. Fourth, it's just not good business.

∾ Wanting to Have Sex with a Subordinate ∾

Well this one is OK. How about that? You can want to have sex with whomever you like. Only one thing, if it's a subordinate, don't do it. If it's someone you work with on an ongoing basis, you shouldn't do it. If it is someone who works at your company, but not directly with you or in your management chain, then assuming it is allowed by the company, be respectful and watch your step.

This whole section wasn't any fun to write and probably wasn't much fun to read. I kept saying "don't do this" and "don't do that." These are all serious transgressions that could hurt you professionally and personally, as well as hurt other people. But that's precisely why it's important to discuss them.

∾ **Key Points** ∾

❈ The advice for this chapter is "No, don't do it." I know that some of it sounds like fun, but don't do it.

❈ As the manager, you must treat all your subordinates fairly and equally. If you don't, the other members of your team will resent it.

❈ Don't gossip about the people who work for you. When you gossip about your staff, others take it as fact not as gossip.

❈ If you don't want your staff to lie to you, then don't lie to them.

❈ As manager of the group, you set the department's mood, rules, and common practices. If you're honest and hardworking, your group will be honest and hardworking.

❈ If you lie to your boss, you very possibly will lose your job.

❈ If you want to get sued or fired, then lie to HR.

❈ As a manager, you will be handling data about people inside your own company. Make sure you handle internal company data very carefully.

❈ When you promise something to an employee, they take it as a done deal. If you can't deliver, then at best, you have lost credibility; at worst, the employee will be on his way to HR to complain.

❈ As a manager, you're in a position of power over your subordinates. Be very careful and respectful as to what you say, what you do, and what you imply. A sexual harassment complaint against you will, at a minimum, be very embarrassing and seem to follow you through your career. At worst, you will be fired, sued, and disgraced.

❈ Off-color jokes have an interesting way of unexpectedly offending people.

❈ No matter how much you want to date a subordinate, don't do it. Unless you live happily ever after, then life in the office may become very uncomfortable.

❈ It's OK to want to have sex with a subordinate, just don't do it.

CHAPTER 12

PERSONAL GROWTH

∼ Make Sure You Want to Be a Manager ∼

Most people go to school to learn a specific profession that interests them. Then over time, as they gain expertise, experience, and an understanding of their profession and industry, they are asked to do something totally different, namely, manage people.

As a manager, you will still be involved in the work your department is doing, but it will be different. Now, instead of doing the work, you will be managing people and overseeing the work performed by your team. It's important that you understand that managing is very different from doing. Furthermore, you should make the conscience decision that you would rather be a manager than an individual contributor.

Throughout this book, you've been learning about your new responsibilities as a manager. What hasn't been discussed is what you have to stop doing, namely, your old job. You can no longer do your old job, which causes issues that are not immediately apparent. Over time, particularly if you are in a technical job such as computer programming or engineering, your technical skills will eventually become stale and out of date. This doesn't mean you can't lead the group. It means that without practice and/or additional new technology training, you will not be able to sit down and perform the tasks yourself.

If you truly enjoy the hands-on work and don't have a strong interest in managing people, then moving into a management position may not be the right career move for you. I have seen a number of very talented technologists try management, not like it, and go back to an individual contributor role. Managers generally make more money than the individual contributors, so if you want to remain an individual contributor there is a cost, but there is also a cost to having a job that you don't enjoy.

My goal here is not to scare you away from becoming a manager, but rather to help assure that you are moving in the right direction professionally.

∼ Defining Your Management Style ∼

What kind of manager do you want to become? Do you want to dig deeply into the details? Do you want to be a visionary who only gets involved at a high level? Do you want to drive your people as hard as possible? Do you want to make sure your staff has a good work/life balance? Do you want your staff to like you, be afraid of you, hate you, respect you, and/or want to be you? The answers to these questions will be partially based on your personal beliefs, abilities, temperament, and values. Other answers will be based on the conscious decisions you make as to how you want to manage.

Many great books discuss management practices and techniques. In general, these books recommend that you provide leadership, give direction, provide encouragement, delegate responsibility, give constructive criticism, and continually communicate. You and you alone must decide if you want to take the time and effort to learn from these books and employ their techniques. Everyone has their own strengths and weaknesses. Therefore, some of the suggested management practices will be easier or harder for you to adopt. That said, through effort, I believe almost any person can employ almost any management technique if they put their mind to it.

Over time, you may see your management style evolve. You may start out very strict and overbearing and years later become mentoring and supportive. You may start out mentoring and supportive and end up strict and overbearing. Conversely, you may quickly fall into a management style that is successful for you and maintain it through your entire career. In either case, you will see that as you grow personally through your life, you will also gain a deeper understanding and a clearer perspective of what it takes to make a good manager and what type of manager you want to be.

> My goal here is not to push you to be a specific kind of manager. Rather, it is to help you grow into the type of manager you would like to be.

My hope is that you will choose to grow into a manager who is supportive of staff, fair, goal-oriented, and extremely effective and successful. I also hope that if you choose to evolve into an overbearing, dishonest tyrant, that I will never have the displeasure of having you for a manager. (Nothing personal, I just like working for good managers. I bet you also like working for a good manager. Now guess what, so will your staff.)

Wow, this section got a little heavy, even for me.

Oh, by the way, did you hear the joke about the manager who went fishing? Sorry, I actually don't know any good manager jokes. I'll tell you what, if you email me a good manager joke, and I include it in my next book, I'll put your name in the credits. You can contact me at EricPBloom@ManagerMechanics.com.

∼ Watching Other Managers and Learning from Them ∼

Throughout your career, you should learn from the managers around you. This includes your bosses, your peers, and in time, the managers who report to you. You can learn from them all and adjust your management style accordingly. Watch them closely and see what they do right and wrong, and learn.

When observing fellow managers, here are some things to look for:

- ❁ How the manager treats his subordinates and how the subordinates react to it.
- ❁ How the manager works with his peers to get things done and is he successful?
- ❁ What decision process does the manager use? In other words, does he look for consensus, analyze alternatives, go on gut feel, take advice from others, act quickly, base decisions only on politics, and so on.
- ❁ What is the manager's work ethic?
- ❁ How is the manager viewed by his staff, peers, and management?
- ❁ How does the manager act under pressure?
- ❁ How does he act during meetings, and how does he lead meetings?

When analyzing these managers, look at both the general and the specific. As an example of the general, does he treat his subordinates fairly and equally? As an example of the specific, what process and steps does he use to estimate his annual budget?

Just for the record, when I say to observe your fellow managers, I don't mean to follow them around. I just mean pay attention to the way they do things. Also, if appropriate, and if you feel comfortable, ask them questions and use them as a mentor.

I've had the pleasure of working for some great managers over the years. Many of the principles I've discussed in this book are based on what I learned by observing their management styles. I've also worked for some managers who were overbearing, dishonest, obnoxious, and just plain mean. I also learned a lot from them. I learned what it feels like to be stuck working for a bad manager and made mental notes to never be like them.

The main message for you here is to learn by watching other managers. Then, incorporate their positive attributes into your management style. Additionally, watch what other managers do wrong and learn from their mistakes.

∼ Finding a Mentor ∼

A mentor is a person more senior than yourself who takes an interest in you and your career. It can be a family member, a friend of the family, your boss, an old boss, or anyone else. The key is that they can give you quality professional advice and ideally have the contacts and influence to help move you ahead professionally. The proper mentor can greatly accelerate your upward professional movement by connecting you to the right person or providing you with the insight to make the right decision.

> I can't overemphasize the advantage of having one or two knowledgeable, well-connected mentors.

There will be times during your career when you are at a professional crossroads that the help and advice of a mentor can be enormously valuable. Should you take the new job? Should you go back to school full-time? Should you take a promotion even if it also means going to work for a person you don't trust or respect? Do you fire a poor-performing employee if he is the president's nephew? The answers to questions like these can have a major impact (good or bad) on your career. Advice from a person more experienced than you can provide you with the insights to take the right step.

Your mentor should be someone you like, trust, and respect. It also should be someone who can give you good advice. You can get bad advice anywhere. Really good advice is hard to come by.

Lastly, no relationship should be a one-way street. Treat your mentors in the way they deserve, with respect, trust, thankfulness, and friendship. Remember, they are helping you out of the goodness of their heart and because they have taken an interest in your success. Furthermore, they know that because of their position relative to yours that it will be difficult or impossible to reciprocate in kind. That's OK, it's the nature of mentoring.

∼ Leadership Versus Management ∼

Various opinions exist about the differences between leadership and management. In fact, a number of books and professional articles have been written on the subject. My opinion can be simply described:

> Leadership is proactive and management is reactive. The best managers have a combination of both.

A good manager reacts appropriately to management requests, business issues, and business processes. By management requests, I am referring to special requests for analysis, cutting your budget as needed, and other similar activities. Example business issues include dealing with difficult employees, solving disputes with vendors, helping customers, and generally handling unforeseen events. By business processes, I am referring to properly following company and department-level procedures. Company-level processes include such activities as budgeting, salary planning, and performance reporting. Department-level processes encompass the workflow-oriented tasks needed to make a department effective and efficient.

The ability to effectively execute the management side of your job is essential to your success.

The concept of leadership is more of an intangible. Leadership is the ability to formulate vision and articulate that vision in such a way that other people understand it, embrace it, and move toward its reality.

In a company setting, leaders are the agents of change, the internal entrepreneurs, and the risk takers. As you can see, adding leadership to your management role adds an entirely new dimension to your job and to your value to the company.

Leadership in a corporate setting also reveals itself in another way, namely through the respect, loyalty, and trust of your staff. In its truest essence, leadership is the ability to take control and have people who wish to follow. In a corporate setting, effective leadership can be a catalyst that drives department productivity, product quality, and organizational pride.

I should point out that companies need all three types of managers—those who are primarily management-oriented, those who are primarily leadership-oriented, and those who possess both skill sets. What you'll find is that management-only-type managers tend to drive processes and efficiencies, leadership-only-type managers drive change and innovation, and managers with both skill sets tend to do a little of both.

∿ Consider Your Next Move ∿

Now that you're a first-line (first-time) manager, what's next? If you have an answer, then good for you. If you don't, then start planning. It's been documented again and again that people who have well-thought professional goals and plans tend to be more professionally successful.

Now would be a good time to meet with your mentor, or if you don't have one, a professional career counselor/coach, to plan out your short-term and long-term goals and plans.

Once you have an idea of your professional direction, your next steps will begin to become obvious. You may find you need to earn a professional certification or go to night school for an advanced college degree. You may find that you need some on-the-job training or need to meet specified sales goals. The sooner you figure out where you want to go, the sooner you can begin your journey in earnest.

∿ Your Continuing Journey ∿

Just in case you're not tired of listening (OK, reading) about my management philosophies, I have one more. I promise you—this is the last one. (I know I'm right because this is the end of the book).

I believe that life is a journey. During your business life, major projects will come and go, managers will come and go, and companies will come and go. Enjoy the journey, learn all you can, be kind to those you meet along the way, and don't take yourself too seriously. Best of luck and journey on.

∽ Key Points ∽

❁ It is important for you to understand that managing is very different from doing. You should make the conscious decision that you would rather be a manager than an individual contributor.

❁ Over time, you may see your management style evolve.

❁ You will see that as you grow personally throughout your life, you will also gain a deeper understanding and a clearer perspective of what it takes to make a good manager.

❁ Throughout your career, you should learn from the managers around you. This includes your bosses, your peers, and in time, the managers who report to you.

❁ A mentor is a person more senior than you who takes an interest in you and your career. It can be a family member, a friend of the family, your boss, an old boss, or anyone else.

❁ Your mentor should be someone you like, trust, and respect. They also should be someone who can give you good advice.

❁ No relationship should be a one-way street. Treat your mentors in the way they deserve, with respect, trust, thankfulness, and friendship.

APPENDIX

∾ Training Guide with Chapter Outlines and Discussion Questions ∾

This section is designed to assist training professionals and HR general-ists by providing a framework for presenting the material as part of a company's management-training curriculum. Each chapter outline includes the chapter's theme, key concepts, and questions for discussion (exception: the outline for the first, brief introductory chapter, "Food for Thought," does not include discussion questions).

Individual readers will also profit by thinking about the questions for discussion. As a new manager, you're likely to encounter any number of situations, and the more prepared you are, the better.

The book's accompanying website, www.ManagerMechanics.com, contains additional training materials, training suggestions, and links to other high-quality management-training materials and organizations.

∼ Chapter 1: Food for Thought for a New Manager ∼

∼ Chapter Theme ∼

The theme of this introductory chapter is that there is a parallel between the skills needed to parent children and the skills needed to manage adults. It goes on to discuss the importance of wanting to do a good job and the role of respect in the management process.

∼ Key Concepts ∼

❈ Both managers and parents provide praise, discipline, guidance, direction, leadership, and a pleasant environment.

❈ Caring about people in your group and fostering an atmosphere of respect are key components of being a good manager.

❈ Interpersonal skills, business skills, and good judgment are necessary to be an effective manager.

∽ Chapter 2: Management Realities ∽

∽ Chapter Theme ∽

The theme of this chapter is that being a manager is different than being an individual contributor (i.e., worker). You are now part of the company's management team, and as such, your former co-workers will treat you differently, and you will be judged on different criteria.

∽ Key Concepts ∽

❖ Once promoted, your co-workers will look at you differently.
❖ As a manager, you will be judged on your decision-making abilities.
❖ As part of management, you must support senior management's objectives.

∽ Discussion Questions ∽

❖ You have just become the manager of your department. There was another person in the department who thought he should have received the job instead of you. Do you discuss this with the person who did not get the job? If so, how would you conduct the discussion?
❖ Instead of competing for the best assignments within your department, you are now the decision maker, determining who gets which project. How do you decide?
❖ Your department is moving from one part of the building to another. You will have an office. Your staff will have cubes. However, one cube is larger than the rest. How do you decide who gets it?
❖ Senior management sends out a memo describing a new vacation policy, which you strongly disagree with. What do you do?

∼ Chapter 3: Managing Your Team—The Good Stuff ∼

∼ Chapter Theme ∼

The theme of this chapter is that to be an effective manager, you must treat the people in your group with respect and loyalty. This includes being fair, making good business decisions for the right reasons, helping the people in your group work through personal challenges, and having the courage to ask for help from your boss and human resources when needed.

∼ Key Concepts ∼

❖ You are not only the manager of your group, you are also its leader.

❖ You should always make decisions based on what is best for the company.

❖ A trusting and loyal relationship between you and your subordinates is essential to your success and effectiveness as a manager.

❖ Your job as manager is to establish the best environment you can for your people.

❖ Work with your boss and/or HR to solve people-related issues within your department.

❖ Help your employees work through difficult personal and/or health issues.

❖ Be honest and straight forward with your boss about issues and challenges within your department.

∼ Discussion Questions ∼

❖ Your company is doing poorly, and one person has to be laid off. How do you decide who should go?

❖ A person in your department asks for Wednesday mornings off for two months to bring her father to physical therapy. Your company does not allow flextime. What do you do?

❧ You agree that being a good manager includes being a strong leader. How do you lead, rather than just manage your department?

❧ You are having a major issue within your department. Two key people on your team are threatening to quit because they can't work together. What do you do?

❧ As a new manager, what things can you do to motivate your staff?

❧ A project is going poorly. You think there is a fifty-fifty chance that the project will finish on time. Do you tell your boss the project may be late, or do you wait until you are sure it will be late? Why?

∼ Chapter 4: Managing Your Team—The Bad Stuff ∼

∼ Chapter Theme ∼

The theme of this chapter is threefold. First—you shouldn't make promises you can't keep. It feels good in the short term, but is very divisive in the long run. Second—sometimes employees do bad or wrong things. It's your job as the manager to deal appropriately with the situation. Third—employees can cause problems in different ways. Each of these ways must be dealt with differently.

∼ Key Concepts ∼

❖ If you promise something to a subordinate and then can't deliver, you will lose credibility with that staff member and potentially your whole staff.

❖ The simplest and best form of office discipline is constructive criticism.

❖ For discipline stronger than constructive criticism, begin by giving HR and your boss a heads-up.

❖ Don't forget the seven kinds of difficult employees: Sleazy, Grumpy, Lazy, Brainy, Tardy, Dummy, and Troubled. (Memorize this list and you can impress your friends at parties.)

∼ Discussion Questions ∼

❖ You just gave a great project to one of your staff members. Another person in your group (let's call him Joe) comes to you and says, "Mary gets all the great projects. That project should have been given to me." Do you promise to give Joe the next great project? Why or why not?

❖ A person in your group has made a big mistake that may cause the company to lose a customer. This person works hard and has a great attitude but is very inexperienced. What do you do?

❖ You have a lazy employee in your group who does the minimum amount of required work. Other people in the department are complaining that he is not doing his share of the
work. What do you do?

∾ Chapter 5: Navigating Office Politics ∾

∾ Chapter Theme ∾

The theme of this chapter is how to navigate corporate politics as a manager. To that end, it discusses political issues with senior management, peers, and subordinates, as well as the proper use of email within a business environment.

∾ Key Concepts ∾

❉ As the department manager, you should be the number one advocate for your department and the people in it.

❉ Moving from being an individual contributor to manager is like moving from being single to being married. Now, it's not all about you.

❉ Effectively managing up is about communication, trust, standing your ground, producing quality work, and being responsive to all levels of management.

❉ When dealing with your peer managers, be a team player. It not only helps you, but also helps your boss.

❉ Don't put anything in an email that you wouldn't want your boss, husband, wife, kids, staff, mother, peers, customers, and the rest of the world to read.

∾ Discussion Questions ∾

❉ Even though it was never a good idea, you used to share email-based jokes with your fellow team members. Now that you are their manager, what do you do about these emails? Should you just not participate, or stop the department from sending such emails at all?

❉ One of your peers (another manager) asks for your department's help on something that is good for her department but doesn't help your department. Should you help? Why or why not?

❖ You are having trouble with one of your new peers (another manager). Do you speak with your boss about it or just handle it yourself?

❖ When talking about the accomplishments of your department and subordinates, where does good communication end and outright bragging begin?

∿ Chapter 6: The Hiring Process ∿

∿ Chapter Theme ∿

This chapter discusses the hiring process from beginning to end.

∿ Key Concepts ∿

❀ The hiring process is the combination of defining the job, getting permission to hire, finding candidates, interviewing people, deciding which ones you like, and presenting a job offer.

❀ There are many laws and regulations that must be followed.

❀ A job description specifies the job's title, salary, job duties, eligibility requirements, and other similar information.

❀ One of the hallmarks of a great manager is the ability to hire good people.

❀ Decisions related to hiring are very visible and painful to correct if you hire the wrong person.

∿ Discussion Questions ∿

❀ You have two good candidates. One is very qualified, but you don't think she will work well with the team. The other person is smart, would fit in well with the team, but she is less qualified. Which one, if either, should you hire?

❀ What are some of the advantages of hiring a candidate who was introduced via an internal company referral?

❀ If you were to write a job description for your current position, how would you describe the skills, experience, general qualifications, and personal traits required to be a successful candidate for the position?

❀ What are some of the things that you can and can't ask when interviewing a candidate?

〜 Chapter 7: The Good, the Bad, and the Other 〜

〜 Chapter Theme 〜

This chapter covers a lot of material, including giving promotions, parity in pay, giving pay raises, salary planning, span of control, converting contractors to employees, training, layoffs, and firing an employee.

〜 Key Concepts 〜

❖ There are many things to consider when deciding if someone should be promoted.

❖ Parity in pay means that everyone doing more or less the same job should receive more or less the same pay.

❖ Giving raises is not just about the money; it's also about the message behind the money.

❖ "Span of control" refers to the number of direct reports (subordinates) a manager can personally manage effectively.

❖ Contracting firms generally fall into one of four categories: "No Way," "For a Price," "For a Shrinking Price," and "No Problem."

❖ From a budget perspective, training is generally categorized into two types: tuition reimbursement and seminar-based training.

❖ "Hard-skill-based" classes teach a specific skill. "Soft-skill-based" training teaches things such as time management and stress reduction.

❖ There are various types of training, including buying books, web classes, webinars, and CDs/DVDs.

❖ These are lots of rules and regulations associated with firing people.

❖ You should have four primary responsibilities during a layoff: keep your department productive, decide whom to lay off based on the company's best interest, do everything in your power to help the people you laid off get new jobs, and try not to be laid off yourself.

∼ Discussion Questions ∼

❈ You are told you can only give one person a promotion, but two people deserve it. What do you do? Can you promote just one? Do you choose not to promote either one?

❈ You have two people in your department doing basically the same job. One makes $10,000 more than the other person. They each find out what the other is paid. What do you do when the one being paid less confronts you about the pay difference?

❈ You are giving raises to the five people in your department. Your average raise has to be 4 percent. You think that one person in your department will leave if she doesn't get a big raise. Do you take money away from others in your department to give to her? Give her the raise you think she deserves regardless of her thoughts on leaving? Or, do you give her a smaller raise thinking that she is going to leave anyway?

❈ Why is it hard to have more than seven people reporting directly to you?

❈ A contractor working in your department comes to you and asks if he can be converted to an employee. What things do you have to consider?

❈ You have six people in your department who have to be trained in the same technology. What are your training options?

❈ A person in your department does something that is against company policy. You think he should be fired. How do you do it?

❈ You have to lay off two people from your eight-person department. What things do you have to consider when deciding whom to lay off?

∼ Chapter 8: HR and Vendors and Finance (Oh, My!) ∼

∼ Chapter Theme ∼

This chapter discusses how you should interact with the HR department, the finance department, and vendors. Regarding the section on vendors, the goal is to simply provide an introductory overview of the company-vendor relationship.

∼ Key Concepts ∼

❋ To work well with the HR department, be willing to meet their deadlines and involve them early in HR-related issues.

❋ By negotiating well with vendors, you can save the company a lot of money, help meet company goals, and enhance your own career.

❋ A Service Level Agreement (SLA) describes in detail the level of service that will be provided by the vendor.

❋ The key to working effectively with finance people is to understand their world.

❋ Your finance person can give you very valuable advice on the best ways to manage your budget.

∼ Discussion Questions ∼

❋ You hear from a friend at another company that one of your vendors may be declaring bankruptcy, what do you do? Do you talk to the vendor? Do you quickly switch to another supplier? Do you simply inform your boss of the situation?

❋ Your company has been working with a particular vendor for a number of years. Another vendor wants your business and is willing to give you a slightly better price. What do you do?

❋ Is it advantageous to buy the same product from two different vendors? Why or why not?

❋ What do you do if a strategic vendor is not shipping their product to you on time?

❁ What do you do if a strategic vendor is not providing their service on time or with poor quality/results?

❁ How can you work with your HR person to your best advantage?

❁ How can you work with your finance person to your best advantage?

∽ Chapter 9: Process to the People (Right On!) ∽

∽ Chapter Theme ∽

This chapter discusses various HR-related processes, including giving performance reviews, Management by Objective (MBOs), salary planning, and succession planning.

∽ Key Concepts ∽

- ❖ Performance reviews are one of the most important things a manager can do for the people in his department. Take them seriously, complete them on time, and be honest, constructive, critical, complimentary, and sincere.
- ❖ When you write someone's review, make sure to discuss both their good points and their bad points.
- ❖ Make sure that your MBOs are consistent with your boss's MBOs and your subordinate's MBOs. If they are, your MBOs will be a lot easier to make.
- ❖ Salary-planning fundamentals include "job descriptions," "job levels," "salary ranges," "salary surveys," and "position in salary range."
- ❖ If you can't be replaced, then you can't be promoted.
- ❖ If done correctly, succession planning is a company-wide activity.

∽ Discussion Questions ∽

- ❖ You are writing the performance review for a person who has done a good job, but whom you don't like as a person. Do you write their review in a positive or negative manner?
- ❖ Should you include constructive criticism and personal improvement suggestions within someone's review or just state the facts?
- ❖ You have a great person working for you. On her performance review, do you just give her a perfect on everything or try to point out at least one area for growth or performance?

❧ Which do you think is harder to write, a performance review for someone doing really well or someone who is doing very poorly? Why?

❧ Should a person's performance review have a direct effect on their pay raise? Why or why not?

❧ If you had to define MBOs for you and your staff, what would they be?

❧ Why is it important that your boss's MBOs, your MBOs, and your staff's MBOs be consistent?

❧ If you have a person in your group who is being paid at a level dramatically below or above their job description, what do you do?

❧ When picking a successor for yourself as part of the succession planning process, what traits would your successor have to have?

∾ Chapter 10: Budgeting ∾

∾ Chapter Theme ∾

This section takes a very narrow view of budgeting. It specifically concentrates on the issues, responsibilities, and activities of a cost-center manager.

∾ Key Concepts ∾

❖ The items in your department's budget can be categorized into one of three types: "No Control," "Some Control," and "Full Control."

❖ Many managers try to pad their budgets with a certain amount of unplanned but plausible expenses so they can meet unexpected business challenges without totally messing up their budgets.

❖ A company can spend money in one of two ways, either for use in the current period (expense) or as a long-term investment (capitalization).

∾ Discussion Questions ∾

❖ What items within your department's budget can you control?

❖ What items within your budget are out of your control? And why?

❖ Do you feel that it is appropriate to pad your budget? Why or why not?

❖ Why is budgeting important and do you think that you should be held accountable for spending less or more than your budget?

❖ How does the budget process work within your company?

❖ You have just become the department manager. You have reviewed your department's budget, and you don't think that it is large enough to meet your department's annual goals and commitments. What do you do? Why?

❖ You have just become the department manager. You have reviewed your department's budget and believe that it includes a number of items that are simply there to pad the budget. Do you try to be as realistic as possible and remove these items from budget, or leave them there in case you are wrong and have underestimated future expenses? Why?

∼ Chapter 11: Management No-No's ∼

∼ Chapter Theme ∼

This chapter discusses all (or at least most) of the things you should not do as a manager. Most of these things you should not do even as an individual contributor, but as a manager, the difficulties are magnified. These topics include picking favorites, office gossip, dishonesty, off-color jokes, sexual harassment, and other similar topics.

∼ Key Concepts ∼

❧ Managers must treat all subordinates fairly and equally.

❧ Don't gossip about the people who work for you.

❧ If you don't want your staff to lie to you, then don't lie to them.

❧ The manager of the group sets the department's mood, rules, and common practices.

❧ If you lie to your boss, you very possibly will lose your job.

❧ If you want to get sued or fired, then lie to HR.

❧ Handle data about your people very carefully.

❧ When you promise something to an employee, they take it as a done deal.

❧ Managers are in a position of power over subordinates and must be careful and respectful as to what they say to their subordinates.

❧ Off-color jokes have an interesting way of unexpectedly offending people.

❧ It's a bad idea to date a subordinate and most likely against company policy.

∼ Discussion Questions ∼

❧ As the new department manager, one of your best friends is now working for you. At the office, should you treat him the same as everyone else in your department, or is it acceptable to give him special treatment? Why or why not?

❈ You hear a really funny and embarrassing story about one of the people who works for you. Do you share it with the other people in your department and others in the company? If you said yes, what kind of stories do you think are all right to talk about and which ones should be kept confidential?

❈ Should you ever lie to your boss? Why or why not? If yes, then under what circumstances?

❈ Should you ever lie to a subordinate? Why or why not? If yes, then under what circumstances?

❈ You left a subordinate's performance review sitting on your desk. You come back to your office and you see someone else in your group reading it. What do you do?

❈ Before you were the department manager, you used to see one member of your team sexually harassing a co-worker. As a peer within the group, you didn't feel that it was your place to comment on or correct the situation. As manager, now what do you do?

⌇ Chapter 12: Personal Growth ⌇

⌇ Chapter Theme ⌇

This chapter discusses the career and future of the manager herself rather than management-related skills. More specifically, it discusses how to decide whether or not you really want to be a manager, how to learn management skills by watching others, and the difference between leadership and management.

⌇ Key Concepts ⌇

- ❁ Managing is very different from doing.
- ❁ Managers need to define a personal management style.
- ❁ Learn by watching other managers.
- ❁ A mentor is a more senior person interested in you and your career.
- ❁ A mentor should be someone you like, trust, and respect.
- ❁ Treat your mentors in the way they deserve, with respect, trust, thankfulness, and friendship.
- ❁ Leadership is proactive and management is reactive. The best managers have a combination of both.

⌇ Discussion Questions ⌇

- ❁ Now that you are a manager, do you like it and is it right for you?
- ❁ What would you like your management style to be? Have you had a manager you would like to emulate?
- ❁ Do you think a mentor would help you? If yes, how do you find one?
- ❁ Do you consider yourself to be a leader, a manager, or both? Why?